GREAT SPORTS FEATS OF THE '70s

The decade of the seventies saw some of the most remarkable and breathtaking sports achievements of all time. Pete Rose of the Cincinnati Reds stretched out a hitting streak through forty-four games, young Nadia Comaneci won three Olympic gold medals with her dazzling gymnastics, and Bjorn Borg won the Wimbledon tennis tournament for three years running. Then there were the teams who set astounding records: in football, the Dolphins, in basketball, the Lakers and Trail Blazers. Here are the stories of the great sports feats of the decade and glimpses of the personalities of the athletes who accomplished them.

GREAT SPORTS FEATS OF THE '70s

by Bill Gutman

Photographs

Julian Messner  New York

Library of Congress Cataloging in Publication Data

Gutman, Bill.
Great sports feats of the '70s.
SUMMARY: Relates outstanding sports feats and profiles the athletes who achieved them.
1. Sports — Addresses, essays, lectures — Juvenile literature.
2. Athletes — Biography — Addresses, essays, Lectures — Juvenile literature.
[1. Sports.   2. Athletes]   I. Title.
GV707.G83   796'.092'2 [B]   79-15298

ISBN 0-671-32954-5

Contents

Introduction

THE WORLD of sports continued to grow and prosper in the decade of the 1970s. Not only did the so-called major sports, such as football and baseball, reach new heights of physical accomplishment and financial gain, but individual sports such as tennis and golf also found a host of exciting young stars and greatly increased prize money, and reached a vast number of new fans through television.

For the first time in the history of the United States, soccer became a well-known and growing sport. Soccer, the most popular sport in the rest of the world, now had a well-organized United States league and got a tremendous boost from an extraordinary player from Brazil, the man they call Pele. The sport of boxing also began to reemerge thanks to the continued existence of Muhammad Ali and the tremendous success of the United States boxing team at the 1976 Olympics.

Great Sports Feats of the '70s attempts to dramatize some of the sports highlights of the decade, describing record-breaking performances as well as acquainting the reader with some of the outstanding athletes in a variety of sports.

Of course, it is impossible to cover all the great events of a ten-year period within the pages of a single book. Some may even feel that certain events, teams, and athletes have been unjustly omitted. But because they are not represented here does not mean that their achievements were not as great or equal to those included.

For instance, on the gridiron we look at O.J. Simpson's 2,000-yard season, the undefeated season of the Miami Dolphins, and highlights of Tony Dorsett's fabulous college career at the University of Pittsburgh. But omitting such stars as Walter Payton, Earl Campbell, or a team like the Dallas Cowboys should in no way dim their achievements.

Our baseball chapters focus on Hank Aaron, Lou Brock, and Pete Rose. In no way does that diminish or lessen accomplishments by players like Rod Carew, Nolan Ryan, or Tom Seaver, or such team efforts as those put forth by the Oakland A's, Cincinnati Reds, or New York Yankees.

The same holds true for basketball. Our focus is on Bill Walton and the Portland Trail Blazers, David Thompson at North Carolina State, and the Los Angeles Lakers of 1971-72. Yet there have been a score of great players and great court achievements during the 1970s, both at the collegiate and professional levels.

After that, we'll take a look at hockey, tennis, golf, boxing, gymnastics, and soccer. Obviously, more great things have happened in these sports than could be included here, not to mention great events from still additional sports.

All this serves to show just how much sports activity took place in the 1970s. So while in one sense this book only scratches the surface, it nevertheless focuses on some of the great sports achievements not only of the past decade but of all time. Undoubtedly more and more record-breaking performances are coming in the years ahead.

The Year of
the Dolphins

THERE HAVE been some great football teams in the history of the National Football League. Some have dominated the league longer than others as the inevitable cycle of sports continued. Who is to say whether the 1940 Chicago Bears were better than the 1956 Giants or the 1967 Packers or the 1977 Dallas Cowboys? That's an individual and arbitrary judgment.

However, there is one thing that can be said with total certainty. No team in National Football League history ever had a season to compare with the 1972 Miami Dolphins. All the Dolphins did that year was to win every single game they played, both regular season and play-offs. En route to becoming world champions, Don Shula's Dolphins won seventeen consecutive games. Here's how they did it.

Until 1966 there were no Miami Dolphins. The team was an expansion club, and they weren't even in the National

Football League. They were born into the American Football League, which, at the time, was considered very much inferior to the older, more prestigious NFL. Yet in just six short years the Dolphins were the best team in football. It seems incredible.

The team had a 3-11 record during that 1966 season, playing with the usual expansion formula of untried youngsters, a few mediocre veterans, and some over-the-hill vets hanging on for a last hurrah. Yet the wheels were turning upstairs, where a solid organization was playing a waiting game. They knew how they wanted to build a team.

Before the 1967 season the team drafted an all-American quarterback out of Purdue who they felt could lead them to the heights. His name was Bob Griese, and they were right. Griese became a regular his rookie year and picked up the valuable experience that would make him a poised leader once the team was ready to make its move. The team was 4-10 that year, Griese throwing for more than 2,000 yards and 15 touchdowns. He showed he could do the job.

The Dolphins' brain trust, Coach Don Shula (left) and quarterback Bob Griese. *(Miami Dolphins)*

The two leagues had already completed a merger agreement by then. Super Bowl I had been played the year before, so the Dolphins knew they soon would be part of an overall National Football League. They wanted to be competitive. Once again the front office eyed the draft.

This time they came up with a number of blue-chippers. They drafted fullback Larry Csonka out of Syracuse. The big guy would soon become the most punishing runner in the league. They also got a versatile rookie halfback from Wyoming, Jim Kiick, who would play an integral part in the team's success. Also coming that year were defensive back Dick Anderson, tackle Doug Crusan, and defensive tackle Manny Fernandez. All would play large roles in the future.

The man engineering all this was general manager Joe Thomas, who had a reputation for building franchises. Thomas had a timetable and was on schedule. In 1968 the Dolphins improved to 5-8-1 and finished third in the Eastern Division of the AFL, ahead of a couple of original AFL teams, Boston and Buffalo.

Then in 1969 the team slipped back to the basement, finishing at 3-10-1. It was a combination of injuries, bad luck, and growing pains. Those who knew football could see that the team was actually better in '69 and building rapidly. For that year they drafted defensive end Bill Stanfill, defensive tackle Bob Heinz, running back Mercury Morris and defensive back Lloyd Mumphord. No dead wood there. And two key trades brought guard Larry Little, who was to become an all-pro and the best pulling guard in the league, and also middle linebacker Nick Buoniconti, a cat-quick defender with the savy to become the leader and inspiration for the young and hungry defense.

So more quality players were coming in despite the losing season. In fact, some people were beginning to notice how much raw talent was being gathered in Miami. It seemed just a matter of time before the club exploded. Griese didn't have a good year in '69, either. A combination of injuries and key mistakes hurt him. His coach, George Wilson, was also down on him during the year and that doesn't always inspire confidence.

Then came 1970, the first year the NFL and AFL were in a combined league. The major change that year was the introduction of a new coach. He was granite-jawed Don Shula, who had been the highly successful coach of the Baltimore Colts. Joe Thomas figured he was the man to lead the Dolphins to the heights and went all out to land him. He became head coach, a vice-president, and a stockholder in the team. That's how badly they wanted him, and the investment was to pay off in dividends, and soon.

Again new players flocked to Miami. The draft brought three fine defensive backs, Curtis Johnson, Tim Foley, and Jake Scott. They would join with Dick Anderson to form one of the best secondaries in the league. Tight end Jim Mandich also joined the team, as did linebacker Mike Kolen. Kicker Garo Yepremian was signed as a free agent, and trades brought center Bob DeMarco, tight end Marv Fleming, and wide receiver Paul Warfield. All three were proven veterans who knew how to win. Warfield was an especially valuable performer, a deep threat par excellance, one of the most spectacular pass catchers in the league.

Griese was looking sharp again. Csonka was an unstoppable bulldozer. Kiick alternated with the electric Mercury Morris, always a threat to break a big one. The offense seemed ready.

The team split its first two games that year against mediocre opposition. So that didn't prove much. But then came the upset, perhaps the turning point in the history of the franchise. They whipped the always-powerful Oakland Raiders, 20-13. That was followed by a 20-6 victory over the New York Jets and Joe Namath, and another victory over Buffalo. The team was 4-2.

Two straight shutout losses to Cleveland and Baltimore evened things out, but then the Dolphins went to work. They beat New Orleans, upset Baltimore 34-17, and swept to four more wins. They had taken six straight games and finished the season with a 10-4 record, second to Baltimore's 11-2-1, and they were in the playoffs as the AFC's wild-card team. The Dolphins had come of age.

It was almost anticlimactic when the team lost to Oakland in the first round of the playoffs. But they didn't lose by much, 21-14, and served notice they were coming. The turnaround had been incredible, from 3-10-1 in '69 to 10-4 in '70. But the careful drafting and trading was paying off. The offense could do it two ways, ball control or explode. And the defense, anchored by middle linebacker Buoniconti and the kids around him, was getting stingier and stingier. Except for Buoniconti, they were a bunch of unknowns, and soon picked up the unlikely nickname, the "No Name Defense." But, oh, could they play.

Some thought the team would slip back again in '71, but not this time. They were too solid. They won their division with a 10-3-1 record. Griese had a great year and was given the NEA Jim Thorpe Award as the league's Most Valuable

Speedy Mercury Morris (left), rugged Larry Csonka (center), and reliable Jim Kiick (right) carried the ball behind a powerful offensive line. *(Miami Dolphins)*

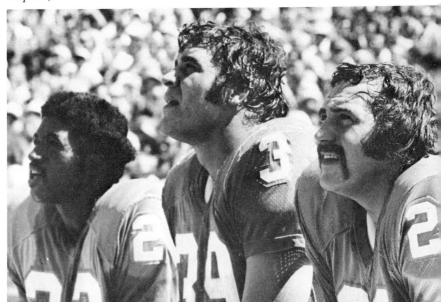

Player. Csonka gained over 1,000 yards for the first time, while Kiick had more than 700. Warfield caught 43 passes for a 23.2 average and 11 touchdowns. Kicker Yepremian led the league in scoring with 117 points and the defense gave up just 174 points, best in the league.

In the playoffs, the team beat Kansas City 27-24 in one of the greatest games ever. It went into a second sudden death overtime before Yepremian kicked the winning field goal. Then they whipped Baltimore 21-0 to win the American Conference championship for the first time. And in just their sixth season, the Dolphins went to the Super Bowl. Here, they pulled up short, losing to a powerful Dallas team, 24-3.

But it had been a great year. Still, despite the fact that everyone knew the Dolphins were now among the best in NFL had to offer, no one was prepared for what would happen in 1972.

The team opened up at Kansas City and fans looked for a replay of the great playoff game of the previous December. But it didn't work that way. The Dolphins blew the Chiefs off the field easily, 20-10. Csonka had 118 yards, Morris 67, and the defense turned back about everything the Chiefs did. They made it look simple.

Next came an easy 34-13 win over Houston. Then the team met the tough Minnesota Vikings. A Fran Tarkenton to John Gilliam bomb made it 7-0 in the first quarter and it stayed that way until halftime. Two Yepremian field goals made it 7-6 at the end of three, but the Vikes drove for a score at the beginning of the fourth quarter to make it 14-6. The Dolphins might be in trouble.

Yepremian made the first dent. He booted a long, 51-yard-field goal to make it 14-9. Now the team was fired up. With minutes remaining, the Dolphins began driving. Griese was cool, mixing his running game with the short pass. With the ball on the 3, Bob rolled to his right and lofted a soft pass to Jim Mandich in the end zone. The Dolphins had pulled it out, 16-14. They were now 3-0.

"We wouldn't have won that game a year ago," said one Dolphin. "That's the big difference this year. This team is growing up. Right now it's hard to see anyone stopping us."

The next week the Jets fell 27-17, as Griese had a big game with 15 of 27 for 220 yards. The team was rolling and returned to the Orange Bowl to meet the San Diego Chargers. That's when disaster struck. Early in the first quarter Griese rolled to his left, looking to pass. He was hit by Charger linemen Ron East and Deacon Jones. Bob went down . . . and didn't get up. He was in pain, holding his right ankle.

"I knew right away something was wrong," said Bob, "but I didn't know what it was. My only concern was how much time I'd miss, whether it would be one or two games, or how many."

Bob was carried from the field on a stretcher, and with him, perhaps the entire season was going out also. Into the game came thirty-nine-year-old Earl Morrall, a veteran who had spent the last several seasons as a backup, first at Baltimore and now Miami. No one knew if he could cut it any more.

But Morrall came in and looked great. He completed eight of ten passes for two scores and led the team to a 24-10 victory. Everyone was happy . . . until word came of Bob's injury.

He had a break in the fibula, a small bone in the leg that runs up from the ankle. And the ankle itself was dislocated. Dr. James Nicholas of the New York Jets talked about the injury.

"A dislocated ankle is a terrible injury," he said. "It's terrible because everything is involved . . . the ligaments, muscles, and the bone. The problem is that so many things are stretched and torn that it's tough to estimate recovery time. And when the cast comes off, the player often has a difficult time regaining mobility."

It was estimated that Bob would be out six to eight weeks, right up to the end of the season. Or he could be through for the year.

Now the team really had to pull together. No one was sure whether they could do it without Griese's leadership and superstar skills. Morrall was good. But he was thirty-nine and hadn't played much over the last several seasons. The next game would be the crucial one. If the Dolphins could win, they'd regain their confidence.

It wasn't an easy game. The Dolphins played the Buffalo Bills and the Bills were up. But Morrall came through when he had to and the defense toughened in the tight spots. When it ended, the Dolphins were on top 24-23, and still unbeaten.

After that, the team seemed to get stronger. Morrall was getting accustomed to a starting role and growing in confidence. He might not be a superstar, but he was a veteran quarterback of considerable skill. He soon began showing his stuff.

First Miami whipped Baltimore 23-0, with the defense starring again. Then Buffalo fell, 30-16. After that, the team steamrolled New England 52-0, then beat the New York Jets 28-24 and the Cardinals 31-10. With Griese on the sidelines the team had won seven straight games and had an 11-0 mark for the year. Talk of an undefeated season was beginning.

There was more good news. With three games left, Griese had the cast off his leg. He was making an unbelievable recovery. There was even talk of his being available for the last two games.

"The leg feels fine basically," said Bob. "I feel some pain when I run on it, but I'm throwing a lot and my arm is great."

Morrall and the defense weren't the only stars. Mercury Morris had emerged as a genuine breakaway threat, and the running game with Csonka, Kiick, and Morris was chewing up yards at a record-breaking clip. With all those ingredients working, the club whipped New England 37-21, then topped the Giants 21-13. They were 13-0 with only the Colts remaining. And the good news was that Bob Griese would be activated for the game.

Veteran quarterback Earl Morrall during his days with the Baltimore Colts. He came to the Dolphins as a backup and did a brilliant job when Griese was injured. *(Baltimore Colts)*

Of course, by now there was no panic. Since becoming a regular, Morrall had been great. He was actually leading the AFC in passing.

The Dolphins wanted the last one. Yepremian booted a 40-yard field goal to open the scoring, then Morrall hit Warfield on a 14-yard TD toss before the half. Two more Yepremian field goals made it 16-0 at the outset of the last period. And the Colts could do nothing against the stout Miami defense. With the unbeaten season about clinched, Coach Shula sent Bob Griese into the game.

Bob finished it out in a conservative fashion, just testing the ankle. It held up. The Dolphins won the game, their fourteenth straight, and were now going into the playoffs with their two quarterbacks.

What a year it had been. Both Csonka and Morris had thousand-yard seasons. The defense gave up just 171 points, best in the league, and the team was loaded with all-pros. Now came the playoffs, and this time the team was determined to go all the way.

In the first game against Cleveland the Dolphins took an early 10-0 lead. But the Browns came back to make it 10-7. A Yepremian field goal made it 13-7, but in the fourth quarter Cleveland bounced back to score on a pass play and suddenly took the lead, 14-13. The Dolphins were in trouble.

By now some of the Orange Bowl fans were yelling for Griese, but Coach Shula stayed with the veteran Morrall. With less than five minutes remaining, the Dolphins began driving. Morrall hit on two passes to Warfield covering some fifty yards. A pass interference penalty then brought the ball to the 18. From there Jim Kiick burst through a hole in the line and ran the ball in. The kick made it 20-14 in favor of the Dolphins, and that's the way it ended.

Now Miami had to play the Pittsburgh Steelers for the AFC championship. The game was in Pittsburgh, and at home in the Steel City, Terry Bradshaw and company would be hard to beat.

Early in the game the Steelers intercepted a Morrall pass and marched downfield for a score. They led quickly, 7-0. Soon it became obvious that the Dolphins were having trouble with the rugged Pittsburgh defense. It was still 7-0 in the second period when Dolphin punter Larry Seiple surprised everyone by taking off instead of punting. He ran for a huge gain and a first down at the Steeler 12-yard line. Seconds later Morrall threw a 9-yard scoring pass to Csonka and Yepremian's kick tied the game at 7-7 at the half.

At the outset of the second half Shula decided to gamble. The team wasn't moving well and he thought they might need a shot in the arm. He surprised everyone by starting Bob Griese at quarterback in the third quarter.

On his second series of plays, Griese decided to load up. He went deep to Warfield and hit his receiver for a 52-yard gain to the Pittsburgh 24. Six plays later Jim Kiick scored.

Since Pittsburgh had kicked a field goal early in the third; the TD and extra point gave Miami just a 14-10 lead. But in the final period Griese had his team on the move again. He marched them downfield and Kiick scored again, making it 21-10. The Steelers came back for a final score, but Miami then held on to win it, 21-17. Now it was on to the Super Bowl. One more win and the Dolphins would really have an unbeaten season. Waiting for them, however, were the Washington Redskins, a courageous, veteran team that always seemed to do just enough to win.

Before the game, Coach Shula made another decision. This time he would start Griese at quarterback. "We're at our strongest going into the game with Bob as the starter and Earl ready if he's needed," said the coach.

Some criticized the decision, pointing out that Morrall was the guy who got the team there. But Shula hadn't made many wrong decisions and most of the players seemed to agree.

"Bob and I have worked together for so long that I feel just that much more secure when he's in there," said fullback Csonka. "Earl's done a great job, but I don't know too many

The dynamic Paul Warfield, one of the game's great all-time wide receivers, was always a threat to go all the way. *(Miami Dolphins)*

quarterbacks who call a better game than Bob Griese."

As for Morrall, there was no kick from him. "I feel I did everything that was asked of me and we kept winning," he said. "I'd like to start, sure, but at this point it isn't a matter of Griese or Morrall. The big thing is to win the game."

So the Dolphins were together when they went to the Los Angeles Coliseum on January 14, 1973, to face the Redskins before some 90,000 fans. Both teams started cautiously. The Dolphins' offensive line was especially fired up. They didn't want the Skins defenders to rough up Griese and were protecting him as if he were a china doll.

Bob completed his first two passes, short ones, with no problem. He looked sharp. Then the Dolphins began driving and he hit Warfield with a beautifully thrown ball for an 18-yard gain. Two runs by Csonka brought the ball to the Redskin 28.

Then Bob faded back again. He spotted Howard Twilley breaking for the end zone and rifled the pass to him. The ball was right on target and Twilley grabbed it for a touchdown. Yepremian's kick made it 7-0 at the end of one quarter.

Midway through the second period the Dolphins began driving again. With the ball in Redskin territory, Griese hit tight-end Jim Mandich for a 19-yard gain to the 2. Two plays later Jim Kiick went into the end zone and the kick made it 14-0.

The second half was a defensive battle. Neither team could penetrate. Griese was playing it conservative by now, trying to eat up the clock with his ground game, and it was working. Csonka was especially devastating, the big man pounding up the middle for good gains.

Washington's only score came late in the game, and it came on a broken play. Yepremian was set to try a field goal, but the snap was bad. When little Garo tried to throw a pass it was batted away and the loose ball picked up by Redskin Mike Bass who ran it into the end zone. It was now 14-7, but the Dolphins kept cool, running out the clock with another long, ground-oriented drive.

So they had done it. The Dolphins were world champions and had done it with a perfect 17-0-0 season. Griese had completed 8 of 11 passes in a great comeback game, and Csonka gained 112 yards on 15 carries to spearhead the offense, while the No Name Defense did its usual superb job. It had been the most amazing season in NFL history.

The Dolphins didn't stop there. They were 12-2 the next year and won the Super Bowl again with a convincing 24-7 victory over Minnesota. Many people felt the 1973 team was even more powerful than the '72 squad. They were more mature, more confident, and had Bob Griese all the way.

But no one who participated in and watched the 1972 season will ever forget it. Sure, you need some breaks to go unbeaten, but it was more than that. It was a team that had been a loser just three years earlier, a team that won without its star quarterback, a team that had a valiant, gambling coach, a team that had caught the fancy of the football public.

In 1972 the Dolphins were kings of the hill, and they'd done it in a way that may never be done again. It had to be one of the great sports events of the 1970s or of any time.

All-pro offensive guard Larry Little was a mighty force leading the runners on sweeps. *(Miami Dolphins)*

The Juice
Goes for 2,000

PRO FOOTBALL has had its share of great running backs. Going back to the early days, their legendary names remain to be savored, like fine wine. Jim Thorpe, Red Grange, Bronko Nagurski, George McAfee, Steve Van Buren, Jim Brown, Gale Sayers. These are just some of the outstanding ones, perhaps the brightest lights in a galaxy of stars leading to the modern NFL game of today.

When it comes to runners, there have been plenty of good ones in the 1970s. The list is almost endless. Csonka, Harris, Foreman, Payton, McCutcheon, Mitchell, Dorsett, Campbell. Running back has always been a glamour position, as well as an important one, and the supply of great runners sometimes seems endless.

But in the 1970s, one runner has outshined them all, not only by his gridiron feats, but also by the very charismatic personality contained within the great body. His name is Orenthal James Simpson, "O.J." to everyone who watches football games, turns on television, or goes to the movies. For sometimes it seems that the good-looking, articulate O.J. is all over at once, making commercials, television dramas, feature films, and doing sports commentary.

All this, however, is over and above his primary occupation, that of a running back in the National Football League. That is where O.J. has achieved his greatest glory and undoubtedly where he will mark his greatest achievements. Records are made to be broken, so perhaps many or all of O.J.'s National Football League marks will someday fall; but he will be remembered for a number of things, perhaps the greatest of all being his season of 1973. For that year, the man they call the Juice became the first and only player in National Football League history to crack a magical barrier. In fourteen regular-season games, O.J. Simpson gained 2,003 yards rushing.

Perhaps the feat didn't come as a complete surprise to O.J. followers. For the Juice has always been a record breaker, a scintillating runner with power, speed, and finesse, a game breaker who could go all the way on any given play. Yet despite an amazing college career and more advanced publicity than the President, O.J. spent three frustrating seasons in the National Football League.

He was with a weak team that didn't have a good offensive line, and he had a couple of coaches who would rather see him carry ten to fifteen times a game rather than twenty to twenty-five. Most superbacks have to carry a lot to get into the rhythm of the game and get their own rhythm. But when the situation in Buffalo turned around, O.J. quickly showed he hadn't lost any of the magic. He had his first 1,000-yard season in 1972 and the next year turned the football world on its ear with his running.

By now the O.J. Simpson story is familiar to most people. But by way of a quick review, O.J. was born July 9, 1947, in San Francisco. O.J., a brother, and two sisters were raised by their mother, who often had to work and leave the children

O.J. as a member of the
Buffalo Bills. *(Buffalo Bills)*

on their own. Before long O.J. was getting into trouble on the streets, being involved in fights and vandalism. It looked as if he might be headed for real problems, maybe prison.

It wasn't until O.J. reached Galileo High School that he began playing football. The team wasn't too good but there was plenty of opportunity. O.J. had a good friend, Al Cowlings, who was a lineman. As Cowlings said:

"O.J. and I were the heaviest guys, so I made the holes and he ran through them."

But O.J. was still pretty much of a wise guy then. He didn't take football too seriously. One day he was caught in a crap game, dice in hand, when the coach, Jack McBride, walked in. O.J. figured he'd get bawled out, but since there was a big game the next day he'd be allowed to play. Not so. Coach McBride turned O.J. and his friends in to the dean. But he also told O.J. something he'd never forget.

"He said no one was ever going to give me anything in this world," recalls O.J., "and if I wanted something I was going to have to work for it. And he told me if I wanted respect, I was going to have to act respectable."

So O.J. slowly cleaned up his act. He went to City College of San Francisco, a two-year junior college, and became the most talked-about running back in the city. Major colleges from all over the country wanted him. After all, when you average 9.9 yards a carry, you must be something special. So after weighing all the scholarship offers and promises, the Juice decided to stay home and spend his last two years at the University of Southern California, USC.

O.J. made his major-college debut in the fall of 1967. He ran for more than 100 yards in his first game and within weeks the entire nation was aware of the 6-2, 205-pounder with the catchy name. Week after week, football fans from all over were asking the same question:

"How many yards did O.J. get?"

He got plenty. Against Washington he carried the ball 30 times for 235 yards. He got 188 yards against Oregon after coming back from a foot injury. And in the big game of the year against UCLA he ran for 177 yards and scored the winning touchdown on a nifty 64-yard run. He was a threat to go all the way from anywhere on the field.

When the season ended USC had a 9-1 record and O.J. had 1,543 yards on 291 carries, the second-highest total in college history to that time. But the Juice wasn't finished. He still had time for an encore in 1968. When he opened the season against Minnesota with 236 yards in 39 carries and 4 touchdowns, the legend grew some more.

O.J. had a fantastic season and his team remained unbeaten. Fans, teammates, opponents, and reporters just couldn't say enough about him. He was the most exciting college runner of his time. His coach, John McKay, summed it up in just a few, well-chosen words.

"O.J.'s just a fantastic young man," said the coach. "He'll

run as often as we need him to run, and the more he runs, the better he gets."

The stats were unreal. O.J. carried the ball 383 times for 1,880 yards and 23 touchdowns. His two-year stats were 3,423 yards on 674 carries for an average of 32 carries and 149 yards a game. And as a senior he led USC to the national championship, as the Trojans whipped Indiana 14-3 in the Rose Bowl. And when it all ended, O.J. was given the Heisman Trophy as the best college player in the land.

Now O.J. was thinking pro ball. Besides wanting to play well, he also knew he'd be in line to make a great deal of money. As for the O.J. watchers, they figured he'd make it big wherever he went. And wherever turned out to be Buffalo, New York, a cold and bitter place to be in the winter months and a far cry from the sun and glamour of California. But that upstate New York city was the home of the lowly Buffalo Bills of the NFL's American Conference.

O.J. didn't like it, but he had no choice. He signed a contract and reported to camp. But pretty soon there were voices out of Buffalo that made it sound as if O.J. would not be a one-man show with the Bills. Coach John Rauch said it wasn't his style to build an attack around one man and quarterback Jack Kemp said a pro runner is most effective carrying fifteen to eighteen times a game, not thirty times, as O.J. had done in college.

Words like that didn't seem to mean much at the time, but they actually heralded the start of three very frustrating seasons for O.J. Simpson. Not only didn't he get to carry the ball much, but when he did he found the Buffalo line incapable of opening the kind of holes he had always had at City College and USC. Granted, O.J. doesn't need much of a hole, but he needs something. Not even Superman can run in the National Football League with no blocking at all.

There were some terribly frustrating games for O.J. in those early days. For instance, in a game against powerful Oakland he averaged 8.3 yards a carry. But he only got the ball 6 times for 50 yards. Then there was a game against Miami where he got it 10 times, but with little or no blocking could only gain 12 yards. O.J. gaining only 12 yards was hard for everyone to believe.

The Bills finished the 1969 season with a 4-10 record and O.J. had just 697 yards on 181 carries for a 3.9 average. He didn't even win the Rookie of the Year prize. That went to another runner, Carl Garrett of Boston. It wasn't a happy year for O.J. Until now, football had always been fun.

"I didn't enjoy it at all," O.J. confessed. "But I learned a lot. We should have won some more games, but we beat ourselves too often with mistakes."

Things didn't improve in 1970. It was more of the same. In one game against the Rams, O.J. tried hard, carrying 14 times but gaining just 24 yards. After the game, the Rams' all-pro defensive end Deacon Jones expressed his opinion of the situation.

"If O.J. were with us he'd gain about twenty-six hundred yards. He's a heck of a runner, but by the time they get enough good players to go along with him he may be punch-drunk."

After seven and a half games in 1970, O.J. went down with a knee injury. He didn't need an operation, but it kept him out of action the rest of the year. He had gained 488 yards on 120 carries for a 4.1 average. Season number two was again a disappointment.

There was a new coach with the Bills in 1971, but the results were about the same. The team was losing, falling behind early in most of its games and abandoning the run for the pass. In one game he had 25 yards on 14 carries. In another, against the Colts, he carried 7 times and had minus 10 yards rushing. It was rock bottom.

"This was the worst game we played since I've been here," said O.J. "We had receivers open all day, but how can the quarterback throw when he's flat on his back? We started bad and just kept getting worse. I've got to somehow keep my sanity."

The Bills were destined to be a 1-13 team that year. And O.J. had 742 yards on 183 carries, a 4.1 average. There was talk of O.J.'s demanding a trade. But when he heard that the Bills' former coach from their AFL glory years, Lou Saban, was returning, the Juice signed a new contract with the Bills.

"I came out of USC as a running back," O.J. said, "but I just haven't had the opportunities that some of the other pro backs have had. They carry the ball fifty to a hundred times more a season than I do. But with Coach Saban back, I expect a lot of changes around here."

O.J. was right. The Bills were not only an improved team, but Saban emphasized ball control, an offense which enabled the tailback out of the I-formation to carry the ball. That was O.J. In the second game of the season, against San Francisco, the Juice rambled for 138 yards on 29 carries. That was more like it. Two weeks later he had 144 yards on 28 carries against tough Oakland. Then came a 189-yard game against Pittsburgh, a game in which he electrified the crowd with a

Everybody knows O.J. has speed and moves, but he has power, too, as he shows here against Atlanta Falcons all-pro end Claude Humphrey. *(Buffalo Bills)*

twisting, darting, 94-yard touchdown run. O.J. was back. And the fact that the Bills were building a young, aggressive offensive line didn't hurt.

The Bills had a 4-9-1 record in 1972, but O.J. finally had a big year, leading the NFL in rushing with 1,251 yards on 292 carries for a 4.3 average. With a chance to carry the ball more, he had proved he could still produce. Now O.J. saw a chance for more. Before the new season began he called his pulling guard, Reggie McKenzie, and said,

"I'm going after seventeen hundred yards this year."

McKenzie had a quick answer. "Why not make it two thousand," he quipped.

"Why not," said O.J.

The record, of course, was 1,863 yards set by the great Cleveland fullback Jimmy Brown back in 1963. No one had really challenged that standard since. But after the opening game of the 1973 season, it became obvious that O.J. wasn't fooling around any more. The Bills were playing the New England Patriots and O.J. was running hard and picking up yards from the first series.

Midway through the first period he broke one. Two good blocks from his line started it, and two beautiful moves by the Juice finished the job. He was off on an 80-yard touchdown romp. Later he broke another one for a 22-yard touchdown run. By the time the fourth period began, O.J. was over 200 yards and there was talk about the single game rushing record, then held by Willie Ellison of Los Angeles, who had run for 247 yards a few years earlier.

With a chance to break the record, O.J. and his teammates kept running. With just about a minute remaining, the Juice took the ball off tackle and bulled for seven yards. That gave him 250 yards on 29 carries. He had set a new single-game record and had started the 1973 season like gangbusters. More importantly, the Bills won the game, 31-13. The run-Simpson-more formula was producing dividends.

People couldn't say enough about O.J. New England

coach Chuck Fairbanks said that O.J. "looked like Grant going through Richmond. We were helpless. We couldn't slow him down. We'd have a hole blocked up, but O.J.'s natural ability would get him away."

And linebacker Edgar Chandler said, "He's even faster than he looks. You think you have the angle on him, then suddenly he's gone. It's really embarrassing."

As for O.J., he praised his offensive line, saying they were blowing the other guys out. But now the trick was for both O.J. and the offensive line to sustain. He couldn't gain 250 yards every week and he knew it. But he did get 103 the next game and 123 against the Jets the week after. When that one was over, Jet linebacker Ralph Baker joined the growing chorus in praise of O.J.

"It seems that everything on him moves," said Baker. "He moves his head, he moves his hips, he moves his legs, he moves his shoulders. A lot of times I knew where the play was coming and I could get the angle. But then you still have to tackle him. And no one can do that alone."

It began to look as if O.J.'s motor was in high gear. He rambled for 171 yards against the Eagles, then 166 against Baltimore. Miami held him to a 55-yard game, but he bounced right back with 157 against Kansas City. He had a huge lead over his nearest rivals in the rushing race, so if he remained healthy, a second rushing title was just about academic. Therefore, the new overriding question! Could he break Jimmy Brown's mark?

Whether they were Buffalo fans or not, most people were pulling for the Juice. He was not only one of the best athletes of his time, but one of the most popular as well. His college coach, John McKay, once said, for instance:

"O.J. isn't only the finest player I've ever coached, but he's the finest human being as well."

And Lou Saban, his coach at Buffalo, echoed similar thoughts "You don't find too many like him. He's a man, a great team man."

The next two weeks were sort of off weeks for Juice. He had just 79 yards against New Orleans and 99 versus Cincinnati. He'd have to pick up the pace. So he did, with 120 against Miami, 124 against Baltimore and then 137 against Atlanta. After twelve games, the Juice had run for 1,584 yards. There were two games remaining and O.J. needed nearly 300 yards for the record. It wouldn't be easy.

The first game was a rematch against New England. They were the team O.J. gained 250 yards against in the opener. But this game was played on a cold, snowy New England day. The field was slippery, icy in spots, and it was felt that O.J. wouldn't have a big day. But he fooled them. While the others slipped, he glided, where they stumbled, he moved, piling up yards in a big way. When the game ended, O.J. had astounded everyone. He ripped off 219 yards on just 22 carries, getting nearly 10 yards a pop. That gave him 1,803 yards for the year. Now he needed just 61 more to break the record.

The final game was played at Shea Stadium in New York against the home-standing New York Jets. The stadium was packed. Everyone wanted to see if O.J. could do it. It was another of those cold, snowy December afternoons, not the kind most running backs thrive on. But O.J. Simpson is not like most running backs.

Buffalo took the opening kickoff and wasted no time. The Bills marched down the field, covering 71 yards in 12 plays for the opening score. O.J. got the ball seven times during the drive and slashed his way for 57 of the 71 yards. After just a few minutes, he was within four yards of the record.

When the Bills got the ball again quarterback Joe Ferguson called O.J.'s number immediately. The Juice got a big block from his huge fullback, Jim Braxton, and piled through left tackle for six yards. He had done it. He was the new single-season rushing leader in NFL history. The game was stopped as his teammates mobbed him. The fans stood and applauded as the ball was presented to O.J.

But the game wasn't over. Suddenly there was another goal. Could the Juice roll it up to 2,000? His offensive line was psyched and so was O.J. He had carried the football more than any other back in history in a single year, yet he seemed as fresh as an opening day. He kept getting the ball and rolling up the yards. The snow was falling now, but not even the weather could stop the whirlwind from California.

In the final minutes O.J. got his last carry. It was good for another 7 yards and put him at 2,003 for the season. Incredible. Plus the Bills won the game 34-14 to finish with a 9-5 record, their best mark in years.

O.J.'s teammates mobbed him again, and he hugged them. After the game he told reporters he was glad it was all over.

"There was a lot of pressure building up on me," he said.

This was the run in the snow of Shea Stadium against the New York Jets that gave the Juice his magical 2,003 yards for the season. *(Buffalo Bills)*

"And it kept building, week after week. I had a tough time sleeping this week. But all the guys here were great. They kept saying they'd get it for me and they did. Without this great bunch of guys around me I couldn't have done it. Believe me."

Lost in the excitement of O.J.'s 2,000 yards was the fact that he'd gone over 200 yards again in the Jet game, making the third time he'd done that in a season, which was still another record. So were his 332 carries. His average per carry was 6.0, an incredible average with so many carries. So O.J. had finally proved in the pros what all his fans knew when he was in college. He was number one.

O.J. continued to be a superstar runner after that, winning several more rushing titles and continuing to lead the Bills. Unfortunately, the Buffalo team, which finally made the playoffs in 1974, then slid back and never really challenged for the Super Bowl. The Juice hurt a knee in 1977 and had to undergo surgery for the first time. By then he was the NFL's second all-time rusher with more than 10,000 yards in his career. His final goal, he said, was to break Jimmy Brown's all-time rushing mark.

But he wouldn't do it in Buffalo. At the end of the 1977 season he was traded to the San Francisco 49ers. So O.J. came back home. The 49ers have a young team and are a few years away from contending for the league title. That's the one unfortunate aspect of O.J.'s career. He's never been with a big winner or a strong Super Bowl contender.

Yet he himself has always been a winner, a man now considered one of the greatest running backs ever. With the season expanded from fourteen to sixteen games, there is a chance that someone will break his mark of 2,003 yards. But no one will ever forget the year he set it, the 1973 season, when O.J. Simpson ran, and ran, and ran, and. . . .

Touchdown Tony Strikes Again

By NOW, football fans everywhere know that Tony Dorsett is a star running back for the powerhouse Dallas Cowboys. Touchdown Tony joined the Cowboys in 1977, promptly rang up a 1,000-yard season as a rookie who didn't even play full time, then helped his team win the Super Bowl and world championship. What a way to come into the pro game!

And now that Tony Dorsett is a pro and, barring injury, should remain a pro until the late 1980s or so, more and more people will tend to forget the things he did as a collegian. Whereas O.J. Simpson was the college runner of the 1960s, Tony Dorsett was the man of the seventies, putting together a four-year career at the University of Pittsburgh that is unequaled in the annals of college football.

He started out as a 160-pound freshman who was immediately a first-stringer, and wound up as a 195-pound senior who seemed to get better with each passing week. In four years as a starter, he missed just one game, and when he graduated he left behind a myriad of college records.

In those four years, Tony gained 6,082 yards on 1,074 carries, both records. He scored 59 touchdowns, tying an NCAA mark set by Army's legendary Glenn Davis, and his total of 356 points was a record he held all by himself. He had 33 games of 100 or more yards, which tied another record. In addition, he set records for the most seasons gaining more than 1,000 yards (four) and the most seasons gaining more than 1,500 yards (three). And to top everything, in his senior year he led his team to an unbeaten season and a national championship. And when that was all over, he was named the winner of the Heisman Trophy as the best college player in the land.

Tony Dorsett was born on April 7, 1954, in Aliquippa, Pennsylvania, a small mining town which is also the hometown of basketball star Peter Maravich, and not far from Beaver Falls, the town that produced a guy named Joe Namath. Seems as if a lot of great athletes have come out of the steel country of Pennsylvania.

Tony's father, Wes Dorsett, worked for the steel company,

Even in this publicity shot,
Tony looks like a superrunner.
(University of Pittsburgh)

like so many other people in the area. But he wanted something better for his son. He told young Tony,

"Go out and do something for yourself. Don't work in the steel mills. When you go down into the mills you never know if you're gonna come out again."

So Tony looked for other things. Pretty soon he discovered sports. When he went to Hopewell High he began learning the art of running the football. Though still painfully thin, he already had speed and quickness, and the instinct to run to daylight. In other words, he had potential.

By the time he was a junior Tony gained 1,034 yards and scored 19 touchdowns. He was beginning to attract national attention and the college recruiters began coming around. When Tony showed he was even better as a senior, more recruiters came. But in spite of all the promises Tony was hearing, he had it in mind to go to Penn State, a school known for its great running backs. But, ironically, Penn State was one of the few major schools that showed no real interest in Tony. Perhaps they thought he was too small.

Tony finished his senior year with 1,238 yards and 23 touchdowns. For awhile it looked like he might go to Ohio State. But the Buckeyes had a sophomore tailback named Archie Griffin, and as Tony said, "It wasn't that I doubted my ability to compete with him. It was just that I couldn't be sure I'd get a chance and I certainly didn't want to wait until Archie graduated."

Before long, Tony was considering his hometown school, more or less, the University of Pittsburgh. The Panthers had anything but a football powerhouse then. In the nine years up to 1973, the team had a 22-68 record. And the year before Tony arrived, the Panthers were 1-10. But the school had signed a new coach, Johnny Majors, who had a fine football reputation. Tony liked him right away and soon after decided to attend Pitt, which was located just twenty miles from his home. So in the fall of 1973, the Dorsett era in college football was about to begin.

The first game that year was against Georgia. Tony was already a starter, and although the program listed him at 175 pounds, the 5-11 halfback weighed closer to 160. But to the Georgia Bulldogs, he played more like 200. He was fast and shifty, and he had surprising power in his wiry body. He could cut quickly and accelerate very rapidly, popping through the smallest hole with authority.

Although the game ended in a 7-7 tie, Tony had lived up to preseason billing. He carried the ball 26 times and gained 101 yards. That's a lot of truckin' for a 160-pounder, but Tony came out of the game none the worse for wear. When he rushed for 121 yards the following week against Baylor in a losing effort, he began to get national exposure for the first time.

The next week the Panthers met Northwestern. The Wildcats decided to try to hit Tony hard and often early in the game, maybe throw off his timing and put a little of the fear in him. But they didn't know quite what kind of athlete they were dealing with.

It was a 7-7 game in the second quarter when Tony began chewing up the yards. At first he was doing it off tackle, banging away with surprising power for a back his size. Despite some vicious gang-tackling, he continued to ramble. He finished another Panther drive with a 6-yard touchdown run, the kick making it 14-7. Northwestern tied it before the half, but the big news was Tony's stats. In just one half of football he had already carried 22 times for 125 yards, a good day for any back going a whole game.

Rain was falling in the third period and the field was getting wet. Pitt had the ball on its own 21 when quarterback Bill Daniels gave the ball to Dorsett once more. Tony hit a hole over right tackle, broke away from a Wildcat defender, faked another, and headed to the right sideline. Then he turned on the speed and outran the Northwestern secondary on his way to a 79-yard touchdown jaunt. It gave Pitt the lead again and gave Tony 205 yards on the day, which broke the Pitt single-game mark of 200 set back in 1930. And he wasn't through yet.

For the remainder of the game, quarterback Daniels used Tony to control the ball and eat up the clock. He did both jobs well, carrying time and again in spite of all efforts to stop him. The game ended in a 21-14 Pitt victory, and Tony Dorsett had gained 265 yards on 38 carries in just his third varsity game.

It was the most yards ever gained by a freshman in a major college game and resulted in Tony's being named Associated Press and *Sports Illustrated* Back of the Week.

A back injury limited his effectiveness the next week, but after that he was up to his old tricks. In the eighth game he topped the Pittsburgh single-season rushing mark of 964 yards which was set back in 1929, and in that same game became the first 1,000-yard rusher in Pitt history. In fact, he gained 211 yards in that game, against Syracuse, and got more national publicity.

"Yeah, I dig the publicity, all right," Tony said. "I really enjoy reading what everybody's saying about me. I guess people are beginning to find out who I am."

In the ninth game that year, Tony ripped off 209 yards on 29 carries in a losing effort against powerful Notre Dame. But it was the most yards ever gained by a running back against a Notre Dame team in its entire history. Notre Dame coach Ara Parseghian had this to say about the speedy freshman:

"He's a remarkable player. I didn't think anybody could make that kind of yardage against us. We contained Anthony Davis and we didn't contain Dorsett. That speaks for itself. I think Tony should be selected on the all-American team as a freshman."

When the season ended, Tony had 1,586 yards on 288 carries for a 5.5 average. The team had gone from 1-10 in 1972 to 6-4-1 in '73. Tony was the second best rusher in the nation and a consensus all-American, making him the first freshman to do that since Army's Doc Blanchard in 1945. He also

Give him just a small opening, and Tony's speed and quickness will take him through. *(University of Pittsburgh)*

finished 11th in the voting for the Heisman Trophy, which was won that year by John Cappelletti of Penn State.

Tony's sophomore year was not quite as productive. The offensive line had to be rebuilt and Tony had a knee bruise that kept him out of one game and slowed him a bit in a couple of others. Plus opposing teams were constantly gunning for him.

"Tony was a marked man his sophomore year," said Dean Billick, the Sports Information Director at Pittsburgh. "He took a pretty good pounding and he played hurt, more so than his opponents and the press really knew. The kid really has a lot of guts."

There were still a couple of big games, like 191 yards on just 14 carries against Boston College and 168 yards against Georgia Tech. Yet when the year ended Tony had "just" 1,004 yards on 220 carries in 10 games. The team was 7-4, including the game Tony missed. He was seventh in the Heisman balloting and still an all-American. But going into his junior year he felt he had something to prove.

And he started proving it early. He rambled for 268 yards

on 21 carries against Army, scoring 4 times. Once more, he made the headlines. But he had plenty of company in 1975. There was Archie Griffin at Ohio State, Chuck Muncie at California, and Ricky Bell at USC, just to name three other great backs that year. So they kind of split the headlines, taking turns with great games.

In mid-November Pittsburgh went up against Notre Dame, and the Irish wanted to stop Tony very badly. But on his first carry Tony got 14 yards. On the second he faked three defenders and streaked 57 yards up the sideline. Three more first-quarter carries and Tony had an amazing total of 148 yards! It was hard to believe.

The Irish toughened and held Tony to 28 yards in the middle periods. By the fourth period Pitt had a 24-14 lead, but they didn't want to just sit on it. They began giving the ball to Tony once more and he responded, ripping off the yardage as the Irish tried in vain to stop him.

He carried the ball another seven times in the final session for 127 additional yards. And when he left the field two plays before the game ended, it was announced that he had gained 303 yards. P.S. Pitt won the game, 34-20.

"I never dreamed I'd get three hundred yards against Notre Dame," said Tony. "The only time I thought I might get three hundred was against Army. But beating Notre Dame is a thrill in itself. I can't find the words to express how I feel right now. This is a big win for me and a big win for Pitt. Now people will realize Pitt is for real."

Tony had another big year. He was over 100 yards in 9 of the 11 games the team played. He wound up with 1,544 yards on 228 carries for a marvelous 6.8 average. The team was 7-4 and went to the Sun Bowl where they whipped Kansas 38-19, with Dorsett getting another 142. He was becoming virtually unstoppable.

This time out he was fourth in the Heisman balloting, the three other big-name backs ahead of him—Griffin, Muncie, and Bell. And it bothered him. Though it was uncharacteristic of him, Tony finally spoke out.

"I'd have voted for myself," he said. "But I guess I'm prejudiced. Personally, I feel I have the credentials and within myself I know I'm worthy of the award. But after this voting I'm beginning to wonder what it takes to win the Heisman."

He didn't know it then, but in his senior year he would show everyone what it took. He lifted weights in the off-season for the first time and came back a solid 190 pounds and a much more physical player than he had been before. And he came back with clearly defined goals.

"First of all, this is the year the team can really go," he said. "I've never been on an undefeated team before. That would be really something and I think we can do it. Plus I've got to admit I've been thinking about the Heisman and about Griffin's rushing record. Both symbolize being number one. I'm a competitive athlete and being number one means something to me, and the Heisman Trophy is symbolic of you being the best college player in the country."

Griffin's record was 5,117 yards; making him the first college runner to go over 5,000. But Tony already had 4,134. If he stayed healthy and had his usual year, he'd probably break it.

The team started the year by whipping Notre Dame as Tony had a plus-100-yard day. After that they continued to win, moving into the top three teams in the country. Tony was also running better than ever and closing in on Griffin's record. By the seventh game of the year against Navy, Pitt was 6-0 and Tony was very close. This could be the day.

Tony got the ball often that day and was running wild. Pitt built up a solid lead and the countdown began. Finally in the fourth quarter Tony slashed through the line for a good gain, and when he returned to the huddle he was college football's new all-time rushing king. When the game ended, Tony had 180 yards on the day and a career total of 5,206.

"It's been a hectic time for me," Tony said later. "A lot of people want interviews and want me to make appearances, but so far I've been able to deal with it. I'm happy I broke the record and I'd like to push it up where it will stand for a

Tony's teammates lift him to their shoulders after he broke the all-time NCAA rushing record against Navy in 1976. *(University of Pittsburgh)*

long time. But the most important thing for me is still an undefeated season and a national championship for the team."

Some people were already talking about Tony's hitting 6,000 yards. The team had four games left, and Tony would have to average nearly 200 yards a game to do it. Plus he was still in a race for the Heisman with Ricky Bell of USC. Bell had gained 347 yards in a game against Washington, carrying the ball 51 times. He was obviously a great back also.

The next game was against Syracuse and the Orangemen were out to win and to stop Dorsett. For one quarter they did a super job. They took a 7-3 lead and held Tony to minus 5 yards. But everyone knew that couldn't last for long.

On the first play of the second quarter, Tony broke loose for 33 yards. Six plays later he drove 15 yards to the Syracuse one, then took it in. At the half Pitt led 10-7, and Tony was up to 78 yards. But he was really just warming up. In the second half he took charge, ripping off gain after gain, and seeming to get stronger with each carry.

Syracuse actually got a 13-10 lead, but Pitt had the ball on the Orangemen 33. Tony took a pitchout, burst into the secondary, then faked three different defenders en route to the end zone and a Pittsburgh lead. He kept gaining the yardage for the remainder of the game, at one point gaining 28 on one play and 33 on the next.

When it ended Pitt had a 23-13 victory and Tony had another 241 yards, running his total to 5,447 and putting 6,000 within reach. Army came next, and the Cadets had always been duck soup for Mister Dorsett. This time was no exception. Tony ripped off another 212 yards in a 37-7 Pitt victory. That gave him 5,659 career yards. Plus the news from the West Coast was that Ricky Bell had a bad ankle and was under 100 yards two straight games. Even the Heisman Trophy was looking better.

Next came West Virginia. Once again Tony ran wild. He had gained 199 yards by the middle of the fourth quarter when he was thrown out of the game for fighting. But the Panthers won, 24-16, and Tony had run his total to 5,858 yards. Now he needed just 142 yards in the finale against Penn State to reach 6,000. In addition, number-one-ranked Michigan lost its first game, and going into the final contest of the year, the Panthers were the nation's number-one team.

The Penn State game wouldn't be easy. The Nittany Lions always have one of the best teams in the country, and in Tony's first three years at Pitt they had beaten the Panthers. In addition, Tony had never had a really big day against them, gaining just 77, 65, and 125 yards in his previous encounters against them.

"It's always been a dream of mine to beat Penn State," he said. "When I was a senior in high school I really wanted to go there, but they didn't seem to want me. Now I want to beat them and have us come out of it eleven and zero. That means more to me than anything."

Penn State defensive coach Gregg Ducatte summed the game up in rather simple terms. "If Dorsett gets two hundred yards against us, we lose. If he gets only one hundred, we win!"

As usual, both cross-state rivals were up for the game, and at the beginning it was tight and hard fought. Tony's first five carries netted just six yards. The swarming Penn State defense seemed to be bottling him up. But how often had a team stopped Tony early only to have him get his rhythm going and take it to them in the second half.

Pitt also fell behind early when Penn State's fine quarterback, Chuck Fusina, pitched a touchdown strike to end Bob Torrey, making it 7-0. The Panthers got the ball deep in their own territory again. Two more Dorsett carries got just 5 yards. Then on third and five Pitt QB Matt Cavanaugh hit end Gordon Jones for a long gainer. Cavanaugh continued to throw once he saw the defense keying on Tony. His passes brought the ball to the 13 and a first down. Then Tony carried three straight times, going in on the last one. The kick tied it at 7-7. That's the way it was at the half, with Tony having gained just 51 yards.

In the second half Pitt coach Johnny Majors made an adjustment. He switched Tony from tailback to fullback. So instead of being the deep back in the I-formation, Tony was now the up back. The maneuver seemed to confuse the Penn State defense. Tony was getting to the holes quicker and getting through. He began to gain big yardage.

With 1:37 left in the fourth quarter and the ball on the Penn State 40, Tony ripped up the middle. He went into high gear and blew right past the startled defenders. Before they knew it he was sprinting to the end zone for the go-ahead touchdown. It was a 14-7 game and Tony was now just 10 yards short of 6,000.

It didn't take him long to get the final yards. The next time the Panthers had the ball quarterback Cavanaugh just sent Dorsett at the heart of the Penn State defense. He got the 10 yards and more, and helped his team score a final touchdown and field goal, making the score 24-7 at the gun.

Tony and the Panthers had done it. He had riddled the defense for 224 yards on 38 carries and had led his team to an unbeaten season and probable national championship. In his final year at Pitt, Tony gained 1,948 yards on 338 carries, enabling him to break Ed Marinaro's single-season rush mark of 1,881 yards. His career mark was at 6,082, another of his 11 NCAA and 28 Pittsburgh records.

"Tonight I finally accomplished my dream," said Tony. "I was a little tired out there and it took me a while to get my second wind. But our whole offense seems to get stronger in the second half and that helps me a lot."

Coach Majors put it very simply, "It's quite likely I will never again coach a player like Tony Dorsett." And others all over the country said basically the same thing. He was the best. In December it became official. He was named the winner of the Heisman Trophy as the best college player in the land, getting 701 first-place votes to only 73 for Ricky Bell. There was no doubt about it.

"The award is very symbolic to me," said Tony. "It means a lot to youngsters throughout the country who look up to the Heisman Trophy winners as I did when I was a child. I hope the good Lord will help me live up to such an outstanding award."

But the college career of Tony Dorsett was not quite over. The Panthers went to the Sugar Bowl where they met the tough Georgia Bulldogs. Pitt won easily, defeating Georgia, 27-3. And in his final appearance as a college player, Tony Dorsett gained 202 yards. The way he was playing his final few games, it seemed as if 200 yards was his barometer, not 100.

The game also assured Pitt the National Championship. So Tony Dorsett had achieved all his goals. Barring injury, his pro career may be just as great as his college days. But no matter what happens to him in the future, Tony will be remembered for his years at Pitt, when he was the most dazzling college runner in the country, compiling a record that made all other runners of the seventies second best.

Five in a Row
for Nancy

HER NAME is Nancy Lopez. In 1978 she burst upon the golfing scene as no golfer has before, male or female. As a twenty-one-year-old first-year pro, she totally dominated the women's tour during a better part of the year, and in doing so, brought more attention to women's golf than it had ever had before.

During one stretch of early summer, Nancy Lopez put a stranglehold on the tour. She won five straight tournaments, a new record, and one that will be very difficult to top. In fact, with more and more fine woman golfers on the scene, it's incredible that Nancy could have done it at all.

What made Nancy even more appealing to so many people was her background. Many people still think of golf as something of a snob sport, played by well-to-do people who have always had the time and money to learn the sport as youngsters. This may have been the case once, but certainly hasn't been in many years. However, that old image still holds with many.

Yet Nancy Lopez came out of Texas, of Mexican-American heritage. She was from a hard-working family that never had much in the way of luxury. She learned golf from her father and never had a real golf lesson in her life. Yet starting with a swing that another pro called "a combination of mistakes," Nancy nevertheless took the tour by storm in her first full year.

Her style of play also brought her to the attention of the public. The women have never been the shotmakers the men are. Many saw women's golf as a conservative game where the winner would be the one who made the fewest mistakes, made the most pars, and played it nice and safe. Again, not really the truth, just the supposition.

But Nancy came along to change even that. She was daring, aggressive, a long hitter who went for the cup no matter what position she was in. She played for birdies, even if it meant taking an occasional bogey. And in doing so she was always capable of the spectacular, the charge from behind, much in the way Arnold Palmer did it in the 1950s and '60s. Any everyone knows what Arnold did for men's golf.

Record-breaking Nancy Lopez. *(LPGA Photo)*

Nancy was born on January 6, 1957, in Torrance, California. Her father's family had originally come from Mexico, but Domingo Lopez grew up in Texas and when Nancy was young he moved his family back there, to Roswell, where he hoped to find more work as an auto mechanic.

Domingo and Marina Lopez had just two children, Nancy and her sister, Delma, who was eleven years older than Nancy. Mr. Lopez always loved sports and was quite a baseball player in his youth. There was even a time when he was offered a minor-league tryout, but he said no because there wasn't enough money involved for him to support his wife. He always felt that given the proper chance, he might have been a big-leaguer.

When he was forty he began playing golf and became pretty good at it. By then Delma was too old to be interested, but little Nancy loved to tag along with her father. She was just seven when she first went out on the links with her father.

"He just gave me a club and told me to hit along with him," recalls Nancy. "And he insisted I keep up with him because there were people playing behind us."

Domingo Lopez quickly saw that his young daughter had a flair for the game. He began sawing off his old wooden clubs so Nancy could practice with them. It was up to her to learn on her own, but her family made sacrifices and stood behind her all the way. If she decided to become a golfer, they wanted to be sure she had every opportunity to reach her goal.

The family saved their money so Nancy could have the right kind of clubs and balls. And there were many times when Nancy wanted to help with the dishes and other household chores. But her father and mother said no. Those hands were for golf. Another time her mother had saved to buy a dishwasher, but once she had the money accumulated decided to use it to send Nancy to various junior golf tournaments around the area.

That proved good medicine. Nancy was just ten when she played in her first tourney. But she had been practicing and, boy, did it pay off. She totally outclassed everyone in the two-day event. And that's still an understatement. Nancy won the tournament by an unbelievable 110 strokes!

She was only fourteen years old when the word started getting out. Seasoned pros on the women's tour were getting the word about a young golfer from Texas who was winning amateur tourneys and could hit the ball a country mile. Jane Blalock, for one, remembers.

"Yes, I heard all about her then," says Jane. "They said there was this fourteen year-old who could already hit the ball further than I could and further than a lot of the other girls already on the tour."

No wonder they had all heard about Nancy when she was fourteen. She had just finished winning the New Mexico Women's Amateur Championship for the third straight year. Things were happening fast for Nancy, but she never let them get out of perspective.

For instance, golf always came first with her. But when she went to Roswell High School, she was involved in other things, most of them athletic. She swam, played basketball, dabbled in track and gymnastics. And she helped the boys' golf team to the state championship. But some of her activity caught up with her. She hurt a knee playing flag football and needed an operation. Fortunately, it wasn't too serious and she made a speedy recovery.

From high school it was on to Tulsa University in Oklahoma on a golf scholarship. She enjoyed her stay at Tulsa, which lasted two years. She was the number-one player on the women's golf team, but was getting restless. Her game was strong and she began to wonder how she would do against the pros.

But she spent a little more time on the amateur circuit, cleaning up for the most part. In 1976 she won seven amateur titles, and was a member of the Curtis Cup and World Amateur teams. Then in July of 1977, she decided to take the big step. She turned pro.

The women's tour had been growing gradually. More young golfers were joining and prize money was starting to increase. For years, the women's tour had been something of a closet sport. Sure, there were great golfers around, but not enough of them. The fans didn't come out and the game was considered rather dull when compared to the men. There were no Arnold Palmers, Jack Nicklauses, or Lee Trevinos on the women's tour. In other words, there wasn't the charisma or the rivalries. The game needed a superstar.

Nancy's first pro tournament in 1977 was the biggest of them all, the United States Women's Open. If ever a tourney would make a young pro run for cover, this was it. The big names usually emerged at the top when it ended. As the final eighteen holes got underway, Hollis Stacy was the leader. Right behind her and making a run was Nancy Lopez. Hollis finally prevailed, but Nancy hung on to finish second. The rest of the women were behind her and trying to catch up. They would soon learn that was a familiar position.

In fact, Nancy entered eight tournaments during 1977 and finished second in four of them. When the year ended she had won more than $30,000 and served notice that she would be a force to be reckoned with in the future. Though the Ladies Professional Golf Association wouldn't classify her as a rookie until the next year, *Golf Digest Magazine* didn't waste any time naming her Rookie of the Year.

But Nancy didn't finish the 1977 season in a happy frame of mind. In September, her mother died suddenly following what was thought to be a routine operation. Nancy even left the tour for several weeks following the tragedy. But her mother's death left her with a quiet resolve.

"I was more ready to win after mother passed away," she said.

Nancy's first two tournaments of 1978 were Bent Tree and Sunstar, and both ended the same way. Nancy Lopez won each tourney by a single stroke. And each time she did it the hard way, making a clutch putt on the second-to-last hole. They were the first wins of her pro career. And it didn't take long for people to take notice. The fact that she was Mexican-American made good copy, so in a sense she got more than her share of publicity. In addition, she was charming and good looking, an easy interview.

Plus the two victories had brought notice of her style. She excited the galleries. She took chances. She played to win.

"You have to be aggressive to win out there," she said. "I want to make birdies, not pars. So sometimes I take chances and get myself in trouble. But I never regret playing that way. In fact, I just love the game, love golf, even when I am playing badly."

But that wasn't happening too often in 1978. Even when she wasn't winning she was there. The others began watching her with respect, even perhaps some fear. Because they soon learned that if Nancy was within striking distance of the lead, there was a good chance she'd get it.

Several tournaments later the women were in Baltimore, Maryland, for the Baltimore Classic. Nancy won it, her third win of the year. Then they moved on to the Forsgate Country Club in Jamesburg, New Jersey, for the next LPGA event. Nancy stayed near the top most of the way, but with nine holes left, she was still four shots behind JoAnne Carner, one of the best golfers on the tour.

Playing her usual aggressive game, Nancy took several gambles that paid off. She rallied to tie JoAnne at the end of the round. The two girls then had to play sudden death. The first one winning a hole would win the tourney. On the first hole, Nancy sank a nifty putt for a par four. JoAnne had problems and settled for a bogie five. Nancy had won it, her second tourney in a row, and got a high compliment from the loser.

"I don't think you could have a better champion than Nancy," said JoAnne. "You can see she thrives on competition and has loads of determination. She never quits. She can be in a heavy rough, or behind a tree, or in a sand trap. But she still makes it."

When Nancy went out the following week and won still another tourney the buzzing started. Only a handful of golfers have ever won three straight, and with so many outstanding players on the tour now, it's harder than ever to do it. Only three women had ever won four straight. They were Mickey Wright, Kathy Whitworth, and Shirley Englehorn, all top performers. Now could Nancy add her name to that list?

The tournament was in Mason, Ohio, and a huge crowd was on hand to see if Nancy could win it. By now she had gotten national coverage on television and in magazines. She was no longer an obscure rookie. She was the leading money-winner on the tour and a personality in her own right. Plus she was cool under pressure. The crowds didn't bother her one bit.

From the beginning Nancy just played great golf. She shot a fantastic 65 in one of the rounds, and at one point in the tournament went 41 straight holes shooting par or better. By the last round she had a 5-stroke lead and she held it easily to win number four.

So Nancy had tied the record and had also run her winnings to $118,948. At that point it was more than twice as much as any one of the women on the tour had won. And as soon as she took number four, the talk about number five began. Nancy was the hottest property in all sports. Her schedule became incredibly jammed up. She hardly had time for herself. And she had a new-found recognition that she had never dreamed of.

"I was walking down the street in New York City," she said, "and people were yelling at me from cars. One person even crossed the street to say hello and to wish me luck in making it five."

Even the other women on the tour were talking about Nancy. But they had only nice things to say.

"Everyone has been saying, 'Let's win one, let's knock her off this week,'" said Jane Blalock. "But it's really amazing. There hasn't been any real jealousy of her. I think maybe the girls are all smart enough to realize how much she's doing for all of us."

Kathy Whitworth, once number one herself, said, "Nancy's on a tidal wave and I'm excited for her."

And Carol Mann noted again how much attention Nancy had brought to the women's tour.

"She's a charming girl and her personality really comes across. But she started it all by winning tournaments."

The only sobering note was sounded by Mickey Wright, a Hall of Fame pro herself.

"Never in my life have I seen such control in someone so young," said Mickey. "Nancy's a beautiful person and her success is helping all the girls. I just hope it won't be harmful to her in the long run. I hope there will still be times when everyone will back off and let her be twenty-one again."

But everyone wouldn't leave her alone, at least not until the matter of five straight was settled. It was a whirlwind week, but Nancy seemed to be coping. She even found time to talk about her game.

"When I get psyched up I feel I can do anything," she said. "But I really want to get out there and win. Whatever it takes, I feel like I can do. There's nothing like hitting a solid drive. Putting is a different feeling. I love to putt, love the satisfaction when the ball goes right in the center of the hole."

Finally it was tournament time. It was the Bankers Trust Classic at Pittsford, New York, and needless to say a huge throng was on hand to see if Nancy could do it. It was a three-day tournament and the first two days Nancy did not play well. But she managed to hang close with her gritty determination. Going into the final round she trailed Jane Blalock by three shots. Then on the front nine she caught fire, shooting a 32 and taking over the lead by two strokes.

On the tenth hole disaster almost struck. Nancy's tee shot went out of bounds and hit a spectator right in the head. The man fell over and Nancy rushed up to him, visibly shaken. But the man wasn't badly hurt. In fact, when Nancy reached him he had a twinkle in his eye.

"At least I'll get to meet her," he quipped.

But Nancy was still upset. She took a double bogie on the hole and lost her lead. If she didn't pull herself together she would lose the tournament. So she took a deep breath, relaxed, and came back to birdie the next hole. Then she steadied her play. With two holes left, the two women were tied for the lead.

On the 17th hole Nancy showed her true grit. Her approach shot stopped some 35 feet from the pin. She lined up the birdie putt, stroked the ball, and watched it roll slowly into the cup. The huge gallery let out a tremendous roar. Blalock parred the hole putting Nancy back in the lead. Then Nancy shot par on the final hole to win it, her fifth straight victory, a new record.

Once again Nancy was the most talked-about figure in the sports world. The victory put her earnings over the $150,000 mark. She had won more money than any other rookie in golf history, man or woman. Her five straight victories had been an amazing sports achievement.

Nancy went on to win her eighth tourney of the year a few weeks later, but then her pace slowed. Perhaps everything had been too much. As of October, she had won nearly $165,000, a new women's record for a single season. She was the LPGA rookie of the Year. She had wanted to break Mickey Wright's record of thirteen tournament wins in a year, but that would have to wait.

Still, Nancy's achievement in her rookie year will not be easily forgotten. In fact, it's a record that may never be broken, what with the stiff competition among the girls today. And Nancy should continue to be a superstar for years to come. As she herself has said,

"I feel that's why God put me on this earth, to do what I choose as well as I can."

And Nancy Lopez does it better than most.

A Man
Named Pele

THE MOST popular sport in the world is soccer. Hardly anyone will dispute that. In nearly every country around the globe, more people are kicking a soccer ball than indulging in any other sports activity. In fact, the sport is called football in most places.

But it isn't called football in the United States. That's obvious. There is an American game of football that's nothing like soccer. Then there's the American game of baseball, and the game of basketball. Add to that golf and tennis, and ice hockey. These have been the traditionally popular sports in America. For some reason, soccer has always been way down the list.

Now things are changing. Soccer may never be as popular in the United States as it is in most other countries, but it is well on its way to becoming a major sport in the U.S. The reason for this is manyfold. In the 1970s there was a real effort to organize the sport. A solid professional league was

The man they call Pele. *(Courtesy New York Cosmos)*

formed, many of the world's top players came to America to play, and there was more emphasis on the sport in schools and colleges.

But one event in the mid 1970s served as the major catalyst for the growth of soccer in the United States. It was the decision of one man to come to America to play. His real name is Edson Arantes do Nascimento. But he is known throughout the world as Pele. And he is the greatest soccer player who ever lived.

That may seem like a rather rash statement. After all, there have been arguments for years about the best baseball player, best basketball player, best golfer, and on and on. These arguments can never be really settled, because so many people have opinions. But with soccer, the opinions are just about unanimous. The man called Pele is the best.

He had been in the spotlight since he was fifteen years old. That's when he first joined the Santos team in his native Brazil. Two years later, as a seventeen-year-old teenager, Pele was leading the Brazilian National Team to the World Cup Championship. The World Cup is held every four years and is the goal of every soccer-playing nation in the world. Pele played for Brazil in four World Cup tournaments and Brazil won three of them.

For the next eighteen years; Pele performed for Santos, and in that time his stature as a great soccer player grew and grew. In 1,250 games he scored the incredible total of 1,220 goals, nearly a goal a game, and in soccer that's an unbelievable achievement. But as one longtime soccer writer said:

"The goals Pele scores are often overshadowed by the seemingly magical sequence that precedes them—his uncanny control, his sudden bursts of acceleration, his instinctive positioning, his inventive passes."

Yes, Pele was the complete soccer player. He was born in the Brazilian village of Tres Coracoes on October 23, 1940. His family was quite poor when he was young, but Pele had a good childhood. His father was a soccer player and would often kick a ball around with his son. Pele's first soccer ball was made out of a tangled knot of rags. He was only eight years old when he got his nickname, Pele, and he has often said that he doesn't know how he got it, where it came from, or what it means. But it was his and he would soon make it known the world over.

Before long all he thought about was soccer. School meant very little to him.

"Soccer was the only career I ever thought of," he said. "I went to work as a cobbler's apprentice when I was young, but I was never really interested in that. I wanted to follow in my father's footsteps. I always thought he was the greatest soccer player who ever lived. He just never got a chance to prove it."

Pele was just eleven when a man named Valdemar de Brito saw him play and recognized his talent immediately. De Brito decided to help him and arranged it so he could play on junior teams. When Pele was just fourteen, de Brito felt he was ready. He decided to see if any of the area teams wanted to sign him. As he said many times back then:

"This boy is going to be the greatest player in the world!"

Finally when Pele was fifteen he took him to the coastal city of Santos. Pele tried out, and when the Santos team saw what the youngster could do with a soccer ball they signed him to a contract, gave him a place to live, his meals, and spending money. This was in June of 1956. By September he was playing his first game for the regular Santos team, his team for the next eighteen years.

By 1958 Pele was good enough to score 87 goals during the season and lead Santos to its first World Cup. Pele was a striker, meaning he played on the attacking line and was supposed to score goals. In 1959 another striker named Coutinho joined the team. He and Pele worked beautifully together and that year Pele got 127 goals.

In the 1960s Pele was already known as the greatest soccer player in the world. He was so revered in his native Brazil that he was declared a national treasure, which meant he couldn't be sold to another team. IIe was also becoming the richest athlete in the world, making somewhere around two million dollars a year.

But unlike other athletes, the big money didn't change Pele. He continued to work harder than anyone at his sport. He was friendly to everyone and generous with his time. No one begrudged him the money he made. Opponents and fans in other countries loved and worshiped him almost as much as his home fans and teammates.

During the World Cup tourney of 1966 a player named Eusebio played brilliantly for the Benfica team. Some people began calling him the new Pele and new King of Soccer. But like everyone else, Eusebio knew better.

"I feel that calling me the new Pele is very unfair both for Pele and me," he said. "To me, Pele is the greatest soccer player of all time. I only hope that one day I can be the second best ever."

In 1969, Pele scored his 1,000th goal. The people begged him to play in another World Cup the next year. He had been angered by the dirty play of some teams in the 1966 tourney, but he agreed to play once more. Again he led Brazil to victory, scoring the first goal in the final 4-1 victory over Italy.

By 1971 it looked as if Pele was beginning to tire of international competition. He announced his final appearance with the Brazilian National Team and went with them to Paris where he appeared before some 100,000 fans who were all shouting his name in unison. In July he played in Rio de Janeiro before 120,000 who screamed his name the whole game. It was his very last appearance with the Nationals, and when the game was over he took off his jersey with the famous number 10 and jogged around the stadium as the huge crowd shouted, STAY . . . STAY . . . STAY . . . STAY . . . .

He continued to play for the Santos team until October of 1974, when he announced his retirement. Once again there was an emotional outpouring for the legendary hero who was leaving the game after eighteen years.

What Pele didn't realize then were that things were happening in the United States that would directly affect his future. Since 1967 there had been an effort to make soccer a major sport in America. But the movement was slow. There were two leagues formed that year with twelve teams from other countries brought in to play in one, and ten new teams with players from all over formed to play in the other.

The leagues merged in 1968 to form the North American Soccer League, but the crowds were very small. As in the past, there seemed to be very little interest in soccer. With baseball, football, basketball and all the other sports taking up the calendar year, most people just didn't have room for soccer in their lives. They knew little about the sport, had no national heroes or traditions to look back upon, and didn't care to take the time to learn.

In 1969 the league almost folded. If it had, pro soccer might have been dead and gone for good. But somehow, five teams stayed alive and continued to operate. In 1970 there were six teams, two coming in, one dropping out. By 1971 there were eight teams, with one of the new franchises located in New York. It was generally agreed that the New York franchise, the Cosmos, had to succeed if the league was to stay alive.

The vice-president and general manager of the Cosmos then was a man named Clive Toye. And it didn't take long for Toye to come up with an idea. He thought, what if Pele were to come to New York and play for the Cosmos? He felt that Pele was the only man who could not only put the Cosmos on the map, but solidify the whole league as well. He could give it credibility, and serve as a magnet to pull some of the world's great players to this country.

When Pele has the ball, it's very hard to take it from him. *(Courtesy New York Cosmos)*

Pele was still playing for Santos when Clive Toye spoke to him for the first time.

"I just wanted to tell him about soccer in the United States and how we hoped it would grow," said Toye. "At the same time I wanted him to remember the Cosmos. I told him we'd be back to see him as soon as he decided to leave Santos."

Toye never forgot about Pele. How could he? He kept in contact and at the same time watched the North American Soccer League continue to grow, if ever so slowly. By 1974 there were fifteen teams stretching from coast to coast and into Canada. And in 1974 they had their best attendance ever, averaging 7,825 fans a game. And four league cities were averaging more than 10,000. It was a far cry from the crowds of 100,000 in other countries, but it was a start. Now if only the league had that one catalyst. Clive Toye still felt it had to be Pele.

In July of 1974, Toye made his first real offer for Pele to play for the Cosmos. There was no immediate answer, but with twenty teams set to begin NASL play in 1975, most of those involved with the league agreed that there was more chance than ever for soccer to break through and perhaps become a major sport in the U.S.

And by early 1975 Pele began to show an interest in coming to New York. The word got out, and many reporters and newsmen were after him for a statement. But he kept quiet until he was sure. Then in June of 1975 he made it official. Pele would be coming to New York and the North American Soccer League. And even though he was getting a multimillion-dollar contract to play, that was not his main reason for accepting the offer.

"If an offer had come to me from West Germany, Spain, Italy, or even Brazil," he said, "I would have turned them down. That would be different. But playing in the United States is an exception.

"I love soccer. I've been playing it for twenty years around the world. So why should I not come to the United States and try to help the game? New York is a great place for sports. I really feel if I come here, I could give something to United States soccer."

So that was the real reason. Pele wanted to give something back to the game that had given so much to him. By playing in the North American Soccer League he could showcase his talents and promote soccer as well. Pele had always been one of the most popular athletes in the world, able to get his good will and sportsmanship message across no matter what the language or cultural barriers.

As for his playing talents, well, he was thirty-four years old, at a time of life when most athletes begin slowing down, especially those in a sport where speed and stamina are so important. What if Pele were to suddenly lose it? What if the King of Soccer was just another player?

"I'm in fine shape," Pele said. "I've never really stopped training or playing to some extent. I don't think there will be any trouble."

Pele was not a big man. He was just 5 feet 8 inches tall. But doctors who examined him over the years all said he was an amazing physical specimen. He had an abnormally slow heartbeat, which helped give him his exceptional stamina. He was also blessed with outstanding peripheral vision which enabled him to see things on the sides some 30 percent better than the average athlete.

In addition, doctors said he had very strong feet and heel bones, which enabled him to absorb impact from jumping and high kicks. When he began working out, he showed them he could still run 100 meters in 11 seconds and jump 6 feet in the air. But perhaps it was all best summed up by the doctor who gave Pele a series of physical tests at one time.

"Whatever this man might have decided to do in any physical or mental endeavor," the doctor said, "he would have been a genius."

Well, they were all right about Pele. He still had it. As soon as he began working out, the players could see he was still the

King. One time he dribbled past two defenders and bolted in on Cosmos goalkeeper Sam Nusum. Instead of shooting, Pele just smiled and passed the ball back.

"I think if he shot the ball he might have torn my head off," said Nusum. "I've seen how hard he can kick. You know, until today, I've only seen him on film. But after today I could see he has every move in the book."

In his first exhibition game against Dallas, Pele was magnificent. With the Cosmos trailing 2-0, he made a perfect pass to a teammate for a score. Then, with the game 2-1, he and a Dallas defender went for a high pass. Pele leaped just a little higher and headed the ball on a line past the Dallas goalkeeper to tie the score. Immediately, the large crowd that had come to see him began to shout . . .

. . . PELE . . . PELE . . . PELE . . . PELE. . . .

It was like any other soccer stadium and any other crowd in so many cities around the world. They were screaming for the magical man from Brazil.

Pele played fourteen games in 1975, then played the entire 1976 and 1977 seasons. After that he retired for the last time, but continued to do promotional work for the team, the league, and for soccer in America.

During his two full seasons, Pele played with his old magic. And with Pele to lure others, the Cosmos built the most powerful team in the league. But other teams were building, also, as more foreign players came to the U.S. to play, and more home-grown American stars began to emerge. Ted Howard, public relations director of the North American Soccer League, talked about Pele's impact.

"His impact on the entire league has just been tremendous," he said. "Pele has given the league not only within the country, but throughout the world, a credibility it has not had before. Plus more American kids are playing, about six hundred thousand are in organized programs now as compared to just fifty thousand ten years ago."

As hoped for, the Cosmos franchise became the pivotal

Pele scores another goal and as usual jumps high in the air to celebrate. *(Courtesy New York Cosmos)*

point of the league. When Pele came over in 1975, the team played in small, ancient Downing Stadium on Randalls Island. But in 1977 they moved to brand-new Giants Stadium in the New Jersey Meadowlands. There they averaged more than 35,000 fans in 1977 and even more in '78. And the three playoff games in '77 drew an average of 70,000, with 77,691 coming to one of them, the largest crowd ever to witness a soccer game in the United States or Canada.

"Pele had to be the first," said Clive Toye. "Once he came, the other great players around the world said, 'If he trusts them, I have to trust them too.' "

When Pele first came over, he said that the game of soccer

was bigger than one man. "I can only show the people the game," was the way he put it. "They will decide."

Two years later, it appeared they had decided. "I didn't expect this so quickly," Pele said, looking at one of the huge crowds in Giants Stadium. "I thought it would take a few more years. But everybody wants to come now. The kids bring soccer here and the kids know it is a great game. Without me next year it will be the same. They will still want to come."

He was right about that. The league continues to grow, as does the sport. And while Pele claims that his role was minimal, Cosmos captain Werner Roth, an American player, disagrees.

"There is no way we would be drawing seventy-five thousand fans to Giants Stadium without Pele, the most sincere, helpful, and dedicated man I have ever seen. The guy is unbelievable."

Many, many people agreed. There was another huge crowd for Pele's farewell game on October 1, 1977, at Giants Stadium. The Cosmos were playing Santos, Pele's old team, and he would play a half for each team. The crowd was wildly enthusiastic despite a heavy rain. Fittingly, he scored a goal, the 1,281st of his career. And when it was over, he pulled off number 10 for the last time, as he jogged around the field. Then he spoke.

"I die a little bit today," he said. "But now I am born again to another life. You see, I stop playing soccer because I want to stop, and that is important.

"I am very happy to be here with you in this greatest moment of my life. I want to thank you all. Now I want to take this opportunity to ask you to pay attention to the young of the world, the children, the kids. We need them too much. And I want to ask you because I believe that love is more important than what we can take in life. So please say with me, three times, LOVE . . . LOVE . . . LOVE!"

The tears were streaming down his face. Pele's career as the world's greatest soccer player was over. But his impact on the game would never end. He is perhaps the best-known athlete in the world, and one of the very few who is loved universally.

But as far as America is concerned, the big event occurred in 1975, when Pele decided to bring his skills to its shores and spread his game to the people. That he did, and the game grows and flourishes. Yet when the man called Pele was asked how he would like to be remembered, he spoke not about his achievements in soccer, but of something else.

"I would like to be remembered," he said, "as a person who showed the world that the simplicity of a man is still the most important quality. Through simplicity and sincerity, you can put all humankind together."

That is Pele, a class human being as well as a great athlete. He is one of a kind.

Aaron Hits
Number 715

WHENEVER A long-standing, cherished sports record is broken, it's an event. There really aren't too many records that fall into this special catagory, records set by legendary performers, records that have stood the test of time, records that give an indication of standing forever.

One of those records was the 714 career home runs hit by the one and only George Herman "Babe" Ruth. The Babe set that magic mark between 1915 and 1935. That's a long time ago. And along the way he became one of the most legendary athletes in the history of the country, a genuine folk hero revered by young and old alike until this very day.

Of course, the Babe also set a single-season standard of 60 homers back in 1927. For years it was thought that no one would ever crack that mark. But when a Yankee named Roger Maris hit 61 in 1961, the baseball world did not take too kindly to it at all. In fact, because the league schedule had been expanded from 154 to 162 games, and because

Maris hit numbers 60 and 61 after the team passed the 154-game mark, his record went into the books with an asterisk alongside it explaining the lengthened schedule.

And once the 60-homer mark went, baseball fans looked to the 714. That would never go, many thought. It would always be there to keep the Babe's legend alive, as if the larger-than-life Ruth needed anything like a simple record to keep his memory alive. But anyway, the 714 stood as a symbol to many.

But baseball in the 1950s and 1960s was entering a new, long-ball-hitting phase, and a whole brace of powerful young sluggers were appearing on the scene, men capable of hitting between forty and fifty home runs a year. Still, a guy would have to hit forty homers a year for some eighteen seasons to break the record. Who could sustain a place like that? Who could last that long, especially with jet travel coast to coast, more night games, more outside interests to break concentration on baseball? It just couldn't be done.

One by one, the sluggers of the fifties and sixties began to fall by the wayside. Great home-run hitters like Ted Williams, Eddie Mathews, Ernie Banks, Harmon Killebrew, Frank Robinson, Willie McCovey began coming up short. Even years before they retired, it was obvious they wouldn't make it.

The two most famous and popular sluggers of that era, Willie Mays of the Giants, and Mickey Mantle of the Yankees, were given the best chance to catch the Babe, especially in the mid-years of their careers.

Mantle was a Yankee, like the Babe, a switch-hitter with tremendous power from both sides of the plate. He was over 50 homers twice and, in fact, the year Maris hit his 61, Mickey was right with him until a late-season injury caused him to stall at 54. That was Mantle's problem, injuries. They slowly eroded his skills and robbed him of his power. He had several subpar years and was forced to retire in 1968 after hitting 536 home runs.

A familiar sight, Hammerin'
Hank hitting another one out
of the park. *(Atlanta Braves)*

Mays was another story. The Say Hey Kid may have been
the most exciting player overall of his generation. And he
could hit the long ball, also going over the 50 mark on a pair
of occasions. And when Mantle was already starting to slip,
Willie was still going strong. He reached the 600 mark, the
second player in history to do so, but by then the end was too
near. He struggled on past his fortieth birthday, but retired in
1972 with 660 round-trippers.

While all this was happening, there was another slugger
lurking in the background. He was Henry Aaron of the Milwaukee, and later Atlanta, Braves. But for a while, people
didn't think of Aaron as a slugger. He was a remarkably fluid
ballplayer who did everything well. He hit, hit for average,
drove in runs, ran the bases, played the outfield . . . all with a
quiet kind of grace that attracted little attention. He never hit

fifty home runs in a single season, but was remarkably consistent. He was also a resilient ballplayer who took care of his body and seemed to get better and better with age.

Henry came up with the Milwaukee Braves in 1954, just a few years after Mays and Mantle made their major-league debuts. So he was of the same era. He was a .280 hitter as a rookie, with 13 homers and 69 runs batted in. He broke an ankle in September of that rookie year, and that was the only serious injury of his long career, which spanned twenty-three big-league years.

The fact that Henry, or Hank, as he was often called, wasn't a flashy ballplayer kept him from the limelight. So did the fact that he played in Milwaukee and Atlanta, as opposed to New York or Los Angeles, places where glamour comes naturally. But none of this bothered the soft-spoken man from Mobile, Alabama.

"I know I'm not flashy," Hank once told a reporter. "But I don't try to be. I just play my natural way. It's almost the same as the way I dress. I have good clothes and dress well, but not flashy. That's just my way and I can't change it."

So while Mantle and Mays began making headlines from their first days in the majors, Henry Aaron quietly went about the business of playing baseball. His second year he was over .300 for the first of many times, with a .314 average, 27 homers and 106 RBI's. The next year he was up to .328, but his power was about the same, 26 homers and 92 RBI's. This was 1956, the year Mickey Mantle won the triple crown in the American League. And by this time Willie Mays had played in two World Series with the Giants.

But in 1957, Hank finally hung up some numbers of his own. He hit .322 with 44 big home runs and 132 runs batted in. What's more, he helped lead the Milwaukee Braves to their first National League pennant since the team moved from Boston in 1954. So while Henry finally got some publicity, it was soon overshadowed by the Braves' World Series win over the New York Yankees, a series in which pitcher

Lew Burdette won three games, including a pair of shutouts. But knowledgeable baseball people saw something else that year. They saw that a kid named Aaron had all the skills of a Mantle, Mays, Clemente . . . maybe more.

Actually, Hank had done plenty that year. He clinched the pennant for the Braves with a dramatic, clutch home run. He led the league in both homers and RBI's. And when the season ended he was named the league's Most Valuable Player. He was just twenty-three years old.

Hank also showed his stuff in the series that year. He led the Braves' hitters with a .393 batting average on 11 hits in 28 at bats. He also clouted a triple, 3 homers, and drove in 7 runs. There was little doubt the man could play ball, but he still failed to attract the attention that some of the others did. Perhaps this situation was best described by Felipe Alou, a fine ballplayer in his own right who played against Hank for a number of years before becoming his teammate at Atlanta.

"I never realized how good Henry was until I played alongside him every day," said Alou. "In the outfield he gives everyone so much of the right-field line, yet he gets to every ball hit out there in an easy way."

So Henry didn't attract attention. And as the years rolled past, Mantle and Mays always hit the milestone numbers first, 300 homers, 400 homers, 500 homers. And whenever they passed one of these turns, they got enormous publicity for it. Henry was always behind them, but before long a few people noticed he was starting to creep up. He was a few years younger, but his body seemed a lot younger. As Hank himself said:

"I take good care of myself. I know I'll only go as far as my body takes me. I always come into spring training at one hundred eighty-eight pounds or so and I'm down around one hundred eighty when the season begins."

Hank was not very big, especially when you think of the image of the slugger. The secret was in his wrists. He had powerful wrists and an enormous amount of quickness in them. A right-handed hitter, he whipped the bat around quickly and with great power. The ball just leaped off it, even when his swing seemed effortless.

To show Henry's consistency, it is only necessary to look at his home-run totals from that first big year of 1957 through 1967. They read thusly: 44, 30, 39, 40, 34, 45, 44, 24, 32, 44, 39. He never threatened the Babe's single-season mark, but he never had a real bad year, either. And suddenly, the numbers were starting to come.

The team moved to Atlanta for the 1966 season, and on April 20 of that year, Henry belted his 400th career homer off Bo Belinsky of Philadelphia. Later that year he and teammate Eddie Mathews set a new record for the most home runs hit by two players on the same team for a career. The men whose record they broke were named Ruth and Gehrig. So Hank's renown as a slugger was beginning to grow, ever so slowly.

Then on July 14, 1968, he whacked number 500 off Mike

The immortal Babe Ruth near the end of his career. His lifetime record of 714 homers stood until Hank passed him. *(New York Yankees)*

McCormick of the Giants. That was to be Mickey Mantle's last year and would see him stall at 536. Hank was still just thirty-four years old. It was obvious he'd pass Mantle, and since he was in such seemingly good condition, people began speculating on just how high he could go. And by then, his peers fully knew what kind of a ballplayer he was.

Said pitching-superstar Sandy Koufax, "Hank is the toughest out in the league. There's just no way you can pitch him when he's hot."

And Juan Marichal, Koufax's chief rival for N.L. pitching supremacy in the 1960s, commented, "That man, if he doesn't beat you one way, he beats you another."

And a journeyman catcher named Charlie Lau, who had played in both leagues, had this to say:

"I've seen every superstar in recent years—Mantle, Mays, Kaline, Mathews, Clemente, all of them—and Aaron's the best. He beats you hitting, running, fielding, and stealing. There's nothing he can't do."

And Mickey Mantle himself placed Hank up on a pedestal. "As far as I'm concerned," said the Mick, "Henry Aaron is the best ballplayer of my era. He is to baseball of the last fifteen years what Joe DiMaggio was before him."

In 1970 Henry reached another milestone. He became just the ninth man in history to reach the 3,000-hit plateau for his career. This meant a lot to him.

"That's what I've always wanted," he said. "Now that I have three thousand hits everything else will fall into place—the homers, runs batted in, everything."

And now more and more people were looking at Henry in terms of his homers. Mays was still ahead of him, but fading noticeably. Yet Willie had moved past the 600 mark and trailed only the Babe. Henry had quietly passed everyone else. He was now the third most prolific home-run hitter in the history of baseball. But what was more important, he was still going strong.

At the outset of the 1971 season Hank was thirty-seven years old. But he was about to embark on a campaign that would finally bring him to the attention of the entire baseball world. The first milestone came on April 27. Hank was batting against crafty Gaylord Perry of the Giants. He waited for his pitch and whipped those wrists around. The ball sailed high and deep to left, clearing the fence with room to spare.

Henry Aaron had just hit the 600th home run of his career!

By the end of the season Henry had shown everyone just how good he was. He was rested more now, playing in just 139 games, the fewest since his rookie years. But he had belted 47 homers, his highest total ever, batted .327, and driven in 118 runs. And when it ended he had 639 lifetime homers. Now he was just 7 behind Willie Mays, who was three years older and just about at the end of the line. Willie was to finish with 660, no small feat by any means.

But now everyone finally knew that the man who would

An intense Aaron about to reach another milestone, his 3,000th hit, in May of 1970. *(Atlanta Braves)*

make a run at the Babe was not Mickey Mantle, not Willie Mays, but Henry Aaron. Hank knew it, too. And he finally showed that beneath his calm, easygoing exterior, burned the fires of competitiveness which were as strong as anyone elses.

"I always used to read the names Mickey Mantle and Willie Mays first," he said. "Then Hank Aaron. Well, I've worked pretty darned hard to get my name up front."

On June 10, 1972, the Braves were in Philadelphia for a game against the Phillies. In the sixth inning Henry stepped up to face relief-pitcher Wayne Twitchell. The Braves already had a big lead, and the bases were full. Henry waited patiently as the count ran to one and one. Then he got his pitch. The wrists seemed as quick as ever. Henry jerked the ball into the left-center-field seats. It was the 14th grand-slammer of his career, his 10th homer of the season, and the 649th of his career. That moved him past Mays into second place on the all-time list. Up ahead loomed the specter of the Babe, and now the publicity and accompanying pressure really started.

Henry finished with 34 homers in 1972. That gave him 673, just 41 short of the Babe. Perhaps he was starting to show his age, but it seemed obvious that he should break the mark. And Henry himself knew it.

"Sure I think about it," he said. "I think I can do it if I stay healthy and if I have a strong man batting behind me. That way they can't pitch around me.

"I've been getting a lot of letters asking me not to break the record. They're not vicious letters, but apparently there is so much tradition and sentiment involved with Ruth's record that people don't want to see it broken."

Early in the 1973 season Henry passed the great Stan Musial as baseball's all-time total-base leader. But there was hardly a notice. Everyone was interested in the home runs. And Henry was hitting a lot of them. Even early in the year when he was in a slump he was hitting homers. Five of his first seven hits went the distance.

After the game, Hank tells reporters about the home run that tied him with Willie Mays at 648. *(Atlanta Braves)*

The press began making all kinds of comparisons between Henry and the Babe. Then early in the 1973 season something new appeared. Henry began receiving large amounts of hate mail, most of it racial. Apparently, it was bothering some people that a black man was going to break Ruth's record. This made Henry very angry.

"Right now the mail is running some seventy-five to twenty-five against me," he said, at a major press conference. "Most of it is racial. They call me 'nigger' and every other bad word you can imagine. If I was white, all America would be proud of me. As far as I'm concerned, it indicates something very low in this country."

Henry was also hearing it at the ball park, even his own. Some fans would come to the park and let him have it in no uncertain terms. One time he was even ready to go into the stands after a spectator.

"I don't care if the fans boo me," he said. "They paid their money to get in and they're entitled to it. But I won't take the racial stuff. I don't have to. And I'll tell you something else. All this is just making me more determined than ever to break the record."

The publicity generated by the hate mail helped bring attention to the problem. As Hank said, "What do they expect me to do, stop hitting home runs?" Finally Hank began getting thousands of letters of encouragement from all over the country. And late in the season a special Harris poll showed that just 9 percent of Americans hoped Hank wouldn't break the record. Eighteen percent didn't care, but some 73 percent were pulling for him to make it.

And he was giving it his all. At age thirty-nine, Hank was putting together another great season. By mid-July he was approaching the 700 mark. His average was around .250, but he was clubbing homers with amazing regularity. Only July 21, the big moment came. He belted number 700 off lefty Ken Brett of the Phillies. It was already his 27th homer of the year. There were people who thought at his age he'd be hard pressed to hit that many all year. Now there were more than two months left for him to get the 15 more he needed.

Once Henry reached 700 the media deluge became almost unbearable. Wherever he went, Hank was besieged by legions of reporters and newsmen asking him the same questions over and over. The same thing happened to Roger Maris when he hit his 61 and it almost drove him to a nervous breakdown. The hair on his head actually began falling out. But Henry showed he could handle it. He was patient and polite, answering quickly and quietly and never seeming to get perturbed.

But reporter Frank Hyland of the *Atlanta Journal* told what it was really like to be Hank Aaron just then.

"All kinds of people are always trying to get to him," said Hyland. "Some want stories, others try to talk him into endorsements, and some offer crazy, fly-by-night schemes that only an idiot would be interested in. It's tough for Hank because he's always been a very private person and now he's lost all semblance of a private life.

"It's gotten to a point where Hank can't go into a public place. Even at the ball parks crowds gather everywhere waiting for him. They're right at the exit and he's literally got to fight his way onto the team bus."

Hank did acknowledge that his pressure was different from Roger Maris's in one very important way.

"Roger was under a very strict time limit," Hank said. "He had to do it before the season ended. There'd never be another chance. In a sense, I've got all the time in the world. If I don't do it this season, I'll do it next season. In other words, unless I get hit by a truck, I'll do it."

After he got 700, his pace slowed. It was ten days before he reached 701 and another sixteen days before he belted 702. Time was dwindling in 1973. Then he got back in good groove. He was getting all kinds of hits and his batting average was up into the 260s, the highest it had been all year.

By the end of August he had 706 homers. Then on September 3, he belted two against San Diego. Suddenly he wanted it all this year. He got number 709 on the eighth and 710 two days later. His batting average was up to .288. He was hitting as well as anyone in the league. A week later he popped 711 off Gary Ross of the Padres. There were ten games left.

While everyone was talking about the homers, one reporter who covered the team made another observation.

"While everyone has been watching the homers," he said, "few have noticed that Hank is now batting two ninety. He's been hitting around three fifty since the All-Star break and I don't think anyone in baseball has hit any better. At thirty-nine, he still swings a better bat for my money than anyone in the game."

Five more days passed. On September 22, he hit number 712 against Dave Roberts of Houston. Two more games passed without a homer. The third was rained out and wouldn't be made up. That left two more with Houston.

In the first one, Hank connected against left Jerry Reuss

for 713. But in the final game of the year he didn't connect for a big one. Still, he had managed 6 hits in his final 7 at bats and finished with a season batting average of .301.

What a year it had been. At age thirty-nine he had hit 40 more homers and driven home 96 runs. And he did it playing in only 120 games. He had shown all over again what an amazing athlete he was. The one negative thing was that he was still one homer away from catching Ruth. That meant a winter of endless questions and the anxiety of waiting for the next season to begin.

But it came. And forty-year-old Henry Aaron was ready for the final assault. It didn't take long. The Braves opened in Cincinnati, and in the first inning Hank stepped in against the Reds' Jack Billingham. He watched two pitches go past, then lashed out at the third. The ball flew high and deep to left . . . and was gone! On his first swing of 1974, Hank had tied the Babe, number 714! He got a standing ovation from the large Cincinnati crowd.

Then Hank sat out the second game. He was hitless in the third, then returned to Atlanta where the Braves were to host the Dodgers. The game was on national television and veteran left-hander Al Downing was on the mound for Los Angeles. Hank came up in the second inning and walked on five pitches. The fans booed.

He came up again in the fourth with a man on base. The first pitch was a ball. Downing then tried the fastball, but Hank was ready. The wrists lashed out again, as they had so many thousands of times before. The ball jumped out toward left. It was on its way . . . and gone! Henry Aaron was baseball's new all-time home-run king. He had belted number 715.

At the huge press conference that followed the game, Hank started by saying, "Thank God, it's over." Then he answered reporters' questions one by one, patient and gracious as always.

Hank was to finish the 1974 season with 20 homers, giving him 733 for his career. Then in a surprise move, he was traded to the Milwaukee Brewers of the American League, where he felt he could take advantage of the designated-hitter rule. It was also the city in which he began his great career.

He played two years in Milwaukee. By now age was creeping up fast. He hit just 22 more homers in those two seasons before retiring at the end of 1976. That left him with 755 homers in his great career.

That wasn't all he did. He left a brace of records behind, including a lifetime .300 batting average, more hits than anyone except Ty Cobb, more total bases and more runs batted in than anyone in history. He also played more games and came to bat more times than any other player in the annals of the game. And there were many others.

But the one he'll be most remembered for was number 715. Because in that moment, Hank showed once and for all his true greatness. No one could ever again argue that the slim, quiet man from Mobile was not among the very greatest of all time.

Lou Brock,
Master Thief

AT THE beginning of the 1970s, the best base stealer in the major leagues was Lou Brock of the St. Louis Cardinals. Brock had been amazingly consistent since his first full year with the Cards in 1965. From that year through 1972, Brock's stolen base totals were as follows: 63, 74, 52, 62, 53, 51, 64, and 63.

To most baseball people, the lithe outfielder compared favorably with the great base thieves of the past. Even though Brock had never made a run at Maury Wills's single-season mark of 104 or, for that matter, the previous record of 96 by the immortal Ty Cobb, the consistency of Larcenous Lou put him right up there with the best.

Yet at the outset of the 1973 season, Brock was having his troubles. He had been thrown out thirteen of the first twenty-three times he ran. Lou had always been a ballplayer confident in his abilities, a man who knew what he could do and did it. But for the first time in years he was worried.

"I was almost thirty-four years old," he said. "I figured I was just slowing up, couldn't run like I used to. I remember one game I was stealing and just stopped, stopped cold in the middle of the baseline. There were all kinds of negative vibes running through my head."

There were other people saying it, too. At age thirty-four, Brock couldn't be expected to continue stealing fifty to seventy bases a year. He'd just have to accept it and alter his game to his advancing years. And that might have been what happened, had Lou not talked with Maury Wills.

Wills must have remembered times when he questioned his own confidence as a base thief. So he had some pretty basic and sound advice for Lou Brock.

"Maury told me right out to keep running and not to count the times I was caught. Forget about it, in other words. I took his advice and with my own attitude of being positive instead of negative, it all started coming together again."

It came together, all right, to the tune of a seventy-steal

Lou Brock had plenty to smile about during his record-breaking year of 1974. *(St. Louis Cardinals)*

season, the second best of Lou's career. He had proved he was not slowing up, at age thirty-four he was as dangerous as ever. He could still steal fifty to seventy bases to go along with his fine all-around play. But even with the added drama of the 1973 season, no one in the world suspected what Lou Brock was about to do a year later.

But before going into that, let's take a brief look into the background of Lou Brock. He was born on June 18, 1939; in El Dorado, Arkansas, but he grew up in Mer Rouge, Louisiana, where segregation was a way of life and black people had it very hard. Lou's childhood memories show just how devastating a kind of life it was.

"You grow up insecure about everything," he said. "You grow up ashamed of your nose, ashamed of your mouth, ashamed of your skin. It takes a long time to overcome that.

"When I was a kid I thought everybody was poor. I didn't know there was such a thing as a steady job. I thought everybody had a job for a day or two and then got another one."

It wasn't until one of Lou's teachers made him do some research on the lives of Jackie Robinson, Don Newcombe, Stan Musial, and Joe DiMaggio, that he realized there might be a way out for him, especially when he found out how much money pro ballplayers made.

Of course, hundreds of thousands of youngsters want to be pro ballplayers when they grow up, and very few make it. But young Lou quickly realized he had a talent for sports and he began to work hard at it. By the time he reached his senior year in high school he was a .536 hitter with a future.

Then Lou went to Southern University in Baton Rouge, Louisiana, an all-black school where he had to work two jobs just to pay his tuition. He went out for baseball but the coach didn't even notice him until he collapsed on the field from exhaustion one day, the result of his extra jobs, his studies, and trying out for baseball. Finally given a chance to hit before the coach, he belted four straight balls over the fence and made the team. That was in 1959.

The next year he had a scholarship and proved worthy of it with a .542 batting average. The year after that, 1961, he left school to sign with the Chicago Cubs for a $30,000 bonus. He was sent to St. Cloud, Minnesota, of the Northern League for the 1961 season and promptly won the batting title with a .361 mark, also hitting 14 homers, driving in 82 runs, and stealing 38 bases, using his great speed and very little finesse. Then in 1962 the Cubs brought him up and he was in the majors to stay.

Because the Cubs did not have a really solid team in '62, there was plenty of playing time for rookie Brock. Lou was in 123 games that year and hit .263 with 9 homers and 35 RBI's. His speed enabled him to steal 16 bases. But he was young then. It was still the day of the home run in the big leagues and Lou actually thought his future was as a power hitter. He stole bases because of his speed but didn't think about it or work on techniques.

He didn't really improve in 1963. His average was only .258 and he was having a great deal of difficulty defensively in the outfield. When the 1964 season started in much the same way, Lou was beginning to feel discouraged.

"I was down," he admitted, "I was confused about everything, and the more I got confused, the more I tried to analyze the situation, the more I thought about it. And that just added to the confusion."

By mid-June, Lou was again around .250, not driving in many runs and not stealing many bases. It seemed as if all he was doing was making errors in the outfield. He had fourteen of them already. He figured things couldn't get much worse. Then on June 15, Lou found out something that shocked him. He had been traded to the St. Louis Cardinals for a pitcher named Ernie Broglio. The Cards were in a pennant race and were looking for more team speed. Lou was told he'd be playing every day and was given the left-field job.

Suddenly, Lou Brock was a whole different ballplayer. He was getting hits, igniting rallies, stealing bases, and playing a sound outfield. His new team and teammates expressed confidence in him from the first. They were in a pennant race and they needed him. Plus Lou himself had made a decision.

"When I first came to the majors," he said, "I felt power hitting was where the money was. It took me a while to realize that power wasn't enough. You had to have consistent power and I knew I didn't have it. I didn't have the physical makeup for it. So I had to make a choice. Do I try to develop myself as a power hitter or do I become a pest on the base paths?

"It took the trade to the Cards to force a final decision. When I went over there I took inventory of myself all over again, and that's when I decided to become a base runner."

Lou played in 103 games for the Cards in 1964, batting .348 for them with 12 homers, 44 runs batted in, and 33 stolen bases. Overall for the season he was a .315 hitter with 200 hits and 43 steals. It had turned into a super season, and the Cards won the pennant.

They also won the Series that year, beating the New York Yankees. Lou hit .300 in the Series and drove in five runs. He was already beginning to show he was at his best when the chips were down.

From that point on Lou Brock was one of the best all-around players in the National League. Year after year he was close to or above the .300 mark in batting, and always around the two-hundred-hit level, and was swiping his fifty to seventy bases. He played in two more World Series, in 1967 and 1968, and was incredible in both.

In 1967 the Cards beat the Red Sox in seven games. Pitcher Bob Gibson won three of them and the Series MVP. But it was Brock who was the catalyst. Lou had 12 hits in 29 tries for a .414 average and stole 7 bases, an average of one a game.

The next year St. Louis got the Series again, but this time lost to Detroit in seven games. Tiger pitcher Mickey Lolich won three in this one and was the MVP. But once again Lou

Brock put on a fantastic show. Lou had 13 hits in 28 at bats for a .464 average. He smacked 2 homers, drove in 5 runs, and stole another 7 bases.

Those two World Series performances established Lou once and for all as one of the true superstars of the game. The Cards fell off as a team after that, but Lou continued to do his thing year in and year out. After conquering his early-season problems in 1973, he was once again on top. Though nearly thirty-five years old at the outset of the 1974 season, he fully expected another fine year.

By that time Lou had totally refined his base-stealing techniques. He made it look easy. He never used any flashy or elaborate slides, hooking around the base, falling away, or going in head first. He used a straight-in, pop-up style of sliding, where it seemed as if he was back on his feet almost as quickly as he went down. Yet it wasn't easy, as Lou explained.

"It's been years of practice and torture for me," he said. "First of all you have to learn to read the pitchers. When you can do this you know when to run and when to get your best jump. This also relates to your lead. If you know the pitcher, you know how far you can get off and still get back if he throws over. So it's essential to establish an association with first base. You can't watch the pitcher and keep looking back at the base. You never beat a pitcher by guessing where you are.

"A runner must also work on his initial thrust. He's got to be able to move out and be at maximum speed within ten steps or so. It's a matter of power and thrust and can be achieved through hard work."

So while he was endowed with a great deal of natural talent, Lou Brock also worked to develop and refine the many specialized skills needed to make a good ballplayer into a great one.

Lou also had his own style. One former big-league first baseman compared him with Maury Wills.

The great Ty Cobb set the first modern stolen base standard of 96. *(Detroit Tigers)*

"Lou never seems as intense as, say, a Maury Wills. Maury would get on first and never say a word. You were the enemy, and he was concentrating on getting to second. Lou is different. He'll smile and say hello, maybe ask you about yourself or your family. But as soon as he's ready . . . bam! . . . he's gone."

Even though Lou wound up with seventy steals in 1973, not many people figured he would top that in '74. As a veteran ballplayer he was too smart to put his body on the line for another ten or fifteen steals. At age thirty-five he would undoubtedly be pacing himself much more carefully.

But when the season started Lou was running wild. He was hitting as usual, and was also stealing bases at a record-breaking clip. By midseason, this amazing athlete already had 50 stolen bases. Suddenly everyone was talking about his chances of breaking Wills's record of 104, and at the same time marveling at the way this thirty-five-year-old athlete was playing.

After all, Wills was just twenty-nine when he set the record, and Ty Cobb was twenty-eight when he set the previous mark. And both of them were bruised and battered when they finished their record-breaking seasons. The question remained, could Brock stand up under this kind of pace? And even Wills himself acknowledged how difficult it would be to break the record.

"At the time I broke Cobb's mark everyone was home-run conscious," said Maury. "So the pitchers weren't used to keeping runners close to first and I could get some pretty good leads.

"But after I stole one hundred four, the game kind of changed. Pitchers started working on keeping the good base runners close to first and not letting them get a huge jump."

And Lou himself saw a difference in the catchers from the time he first came into the league to 1974.

"When I first came up there wasn't that much stealing and the catchers weren't ready. Not that many of them could get the ball down to second quickly. And not many throws came in low and on the bag. But with more players running in the last few years, the younger catchers are ready. They can all throw and welcome the challenge of cutting down the top base runners."

But none of that stopped Lou. As usual, his average was up around the .300 mark, so he was getting on base enough, and once on base, he was always a threat to go. As he himself said:

"First base is nowhere, and most times it's useless to stay there. On the other hand, second base is probably the safest place on the field. When I steal second, I practically eliminate the double play, and I can score on almost anything hit past the infield."

So Lou kept running, despite the predictions by almost everyone concerned that his age would lead him to slow down during the dog days of July and August. By August 1, he had 66 steals, though there were signs that he was beginning to slow down.

Then the Cards played host to the Phillies for a weekend

series, August 3, 4 and 5. In four games Lou banged out 10 hits in 17 trips. And it seemed as if every time he got a hit he was stealing a base. He swiped 8 in 9 tries, giving him 74 steals in 109 games. Now everyone began talking of the record once again.

Lou got his 90th steal in the team's 130th game. With 32 games remaining it looked as if only an injury could stop him. Now there was nationwide publicity about the running feats of the great Cardinal star. For the first time in his career he was getting the kind of notices he deserved. He also got something he didn't deserve.

In early September, both Lou and rookie center-fielder Bake McBride, received letters threatening their lives. The letters were filled with racial slurs and written by a man who said he was terminally ill and had nothing to lose by shooting the two star players. Both Brock and McBride were put under close guard.

"I can't say this doesn't bother me," admitted Lou. "Whenever someone threatens to kill you it's real. The fear is there. Both Bake and I have got to try to forget about it."

Like true professionals, both players continued to concentrate on the game, and fortunately nothing more came of the threat. And Brock continued to steal bases. On September 6, he swiped his 100th base against the Mets. And four days later he did it, tying and breaking the record on September 10, with two steals against the Phils. He now had 105 stolen bases for the year.

"I never thought it would happen," said Lou. "But now I'm glad it's over. I can't really say I care about records because I'm not on an ego trip. I just steal to win. But maybe when I'm seventy-five, I'll care."

One man who did care was Maury Wills, the former record holder. Being his usual honest self, Maury told what it's like for an athlete's record to be broken.

"I always felt it was *my* record," admitted Maury. "I didn't think anyone would approach it so soon, not even in my lifetime. I don't think anyone looks forward to seeing his own record broken. So, honestly, I was hoping he wouldn't do it. Of course, once he got around eighty it became obvious. But don't get me wrong. I never wished Lou any kind of tough luck. In fact, my hat's off to the man."

Lou wasn't finished yet. There were still some games to go. He kept playing hard and running hard. When the season ended he had extended his new record to an unbelievable 118 steals in 153 games. It has to be one of the most amazing baseball records ever set, especially considering Lou's age at the time he set it. He also found time to bat .306, get 194 hits, score 105 runs, and drive home 48.

There was plenty of publicity for Lou because of his great feat. But for one St. Louis writer, the drama would have a missing act.

"The shame of it is," he wrote, "that the Cards didn't win the pennant. Because then the entire country could have had the pleasure of seeing Lou Brock perform in another World Series, where his sheer artistry becomes more evident than ever."

The Cards came close in '74, finishing second in their divi-

Maury Wills, the fiery shortstop of the Dodgers, broke Cobb's mark with 104 steals in 1962. *(Baseball Hall of Fame)*

sion. Then, after the season, there was another disappointment for Lou's fans. Steve Garvey of the pennant-winning Dodgers was named the league's Most Valuable Player, with Lou second. But none of that could dim Lou's fantastic achievement.

And he didn't stop there. The next year he batted .309 and swiped 56 bases, which gave him a lifetime total of 809 thefts, putting him within striking distance of Cobb's lifetime mark of 892. Then in 1976, at age thirty-seven, he stole another 56, extending his own record of consecutive years of 50 steals or more to 12.

In 1977, Lou was finally slowing down. But he still swiped 34 sacks, enabling him to break Cobb's mark and finish the season with an even 900 steals. There is little doubt now that Lou Brock is baseball's all-time base-stealing champion.

His consistency and longevity are the things that mark him as one of the all-time greats and a certain Hall of Famer in the future. But even with all that, it was the fantastic record he set in 1974 that will be remembered by most fans. It could be broken someday, but it will take quite a ballplayer to do it. Because it was set by quite a ballplayer, and ranks as one of the great sports events of the decade.

The Streak

THEY CALL the man Charlie Hustle because that's the way he plays baseball. He's played baseball that way ever since joining the Cincinnati Reds as a hustling rookie in 1963. And as the decade of the 1970s draws to a close, Pete Rose has established himself as one of the great ballplayers of all time.

There have been many milestones in Pete's career, batting championships, World Series wins, a Most Valuable Player prize, 3,000 career hits, and a host of other records. Yet in 1978, at the age of thirty-seven, Pete Rose became the focus of the entire sports world as he made a run at one of baseball's greatest and most established records.

From June 14 to August 1, Pete Rose hit safely in 44 straight ball games, breaking the modern National League record of 37 and making the first real run at Joe DiMaggio's cherished mark of 56 straight set in 1941.

Many baseball authorities—players, managers, writers, fans—have maintained that the DiMaggio mark is one of the few baseball records that may never be broken. For a hitting streak is a different thing, and when you think of it in terms of 56 games, more than one-third of the season, it becomes a magnificent achievement.

Pete rarely smiles during a game. He's all business then. *(Cincinnati Reds)*

Why is a long hitting streak so different, so improbable, that many of the game's great hitters rarely put together a streak of even twenty games? Well, for one thing there's an old baseball adage that says good pitching can stop good hitting anytime. In other words, when a good pitcher is having a good day, he's very hard to hit. And the odds favor a streaking hitter running up against a good pitcher on a good day several times during a lengthy streak. Also, there are many more strong relief pitchers around today, so if the starter tires, fresh arms are ready to step in.

And there are other things, such as great fielding plays. As a matter of fact, DiMaggio's 56-gamer was stopped when Cleveland third-baseman Ken Keltner made two tremendous fielding plays. After that DiMag hit in 16 more. Had Keltner not been fielding so well that day the streak might have reached 73.

Other things can happen. A hitter might walk twice and only get two official at bats. A game could be rained out after a hit. The man could come up with an injury. There are so many little things in the game of baseball that cut back the odds for a long streak.

Not to mention the pressure, too. Once the numbers start adding up there are questions, comparisons, constant reminders of what's happening. And the pitchers know it, too, so they naturally bear down just a little harder whenever the streaking batter comes up. Think of all those things and you realize how amazing the DiMaggio record is and how amazing Pete Rose's run at it was.

Though the record is often looked upon as untouchable, there were many who thought that Pete Rose, more than anyone else playing in the 1970s, was geared to break it, even at age thirty-seven. That's because of Pete's attitude and enthusiasm for the game. No one loves to play baseball more than the man they call Charlie Hustle. Every game is a big game to him. He never lets down or tires. He's rarely hurt, rarely misses a game. And he loves the pressure. As the most prolific switch-hitter of all time, he had another advantage, being able to jump from the right to the left side of the plate whenever a pitching change dictated it. Pete is also basically a singles hitter who knows how to handle the bat. A long hitting streak is even more improbable for a power hitter who is always swinging from the heels.

Looking back at Pete's career, it's surprising he didn't put together a long hitting streak before. Born in Cincinnati on April 14, 1941, Pete seemed destined to be a ballplayer all along. His father, Harry "Pete" Rose was a semipro athlete of some renown in the area and Pete was brought up in a sports atmosphere. When he was nine years old he saw a major-league ballplayer who was to have a permanent impact on his life.

"That's when I first saw Enos Slaughter play. He stayed in the majors until he was over 40. They called him the Old Warhorse then, and he hustled right up until the day he quit. He was over 30 when I first saw him, and he still sprinted to first base on a walk. I couldn't believe a big leaguer would do that. He took the extra base whenever he could and once even scored from first on a single and won a ball game. He was an unbelievable competitor, the Charlie Hustle of his day, and I knew right then that I'd model myself after him."

And that's just what Pete did. There wasn't a day in his sporting life after that when he didn't hustle. Though small for his age as a teenager, he competed in football and baseball against bigger, stronger boys and didn't give an inch. He was a switch-hitter already, having begun in Little League at the suggestion of his uncle. By the time he reached high school, football had taken over as his favorite sport. But his size hurt him and he slowly gravitated to baseball, something he hasn't regretted for a single minute since.

"It's funny now," he says, "but if I had known then that I'd grow to almost six feet and weigh close to 200 pounds, I probably would have tried football on the college level. But I thought I'd always be too small and turned to baseball instead."

By 1960, Pete was in the Cincinnati organization and playing in the minor leagues. After a year of getting acclimated he hit .331 and .330, and by 1963 was ready for the majors. He won the second-base job with the Reds in spring training and began his career.

"I love everything about the game of baseball," he said. "Just coming out to the ball park is a thrill."

That's the way Pete played, every day. By the end of the 1963 season he had established himself. He was a .273 hitter and named National League Rookie of the Year. Two years later he really came into his own. Playing in all 162 games he led the league with 209 hits in 670 at bats. He had 35 doubles, 11 triples, 11 homers, and 81 RBI's. He scored 117 runs and had a batting average of .312.

It was more or less a prototype season for him. For he quickly became one of the most consistent ballplayers of his generation. In 1966 he batted .313 with 205 hits, and in 1968 won his first batting title with a .335 average and 210 hits. And in 1969 he repeated as batting champ with a .348 average and 218 hits. He was an established star, almost guaranteed to bat over .300 and get more than 200 hits. And he also showed his versatility by moving to the outfield when Tommy Helms came in to play second base.

Pete's style of play was well known by then, his hustling, head first slides, diving catches. When you're in the limelight there's always somebody ready to criticize. And Pete sometimes would hear or read about someone calling him a hot dog. That kind of stuff always got his dander up, because on the ball field Pete had a reason for everything he did.

"People who say I'm a hot dog just don't know the game or what they're talking about. For instance, I've found that the head first slide is the best slide, a winning slide. It gets you into the base quicker and you don't lose momentum by throwing your body backwards. And there's a lot less chance of a leg or ankle injury sliding that way. As for diving in the outfield, well, I'm past the point of wanting to see my picture in the papers or on television. If I dive for the ball it's because I'm trying for the out. The Cincinnati people are paying me a lot of money and the least I can do is give them everything I have."

That's what he did, year in and year out. And as the 1960s turned into the seventies, Pete became part of a powerful team in Cincy nicknamed the Big Red Machine. In addition to Rose there was Johnny Bench, Tony Perez, Joe Morgan, George Foster, Dave Concepcion, Ken Griffey, and others. They weren't all there at the beginning of the decade, but the nucleus was and the club was powerful. They got into the world series in 1970 and '72, but were beaten both times. In 1973 they lost in the playoffs but Pete won another batting title with a .338 average, 230 hits, and 64 RBI's. He was named the Most Valuable Player in the National League.

The team finally crested in 1975 and '76, winning World Series titles over the Boston Red Sox and New York Yankees. They were acclaimed the best team in baseball, and Pete was one of the leaders. A veteran now, he was a lifetime .300 hitter and was approaching new milestones in hits and 200-hit seasons. He also showed his versatility by moving back to the infield, to play third, so young outfielders Foster, Cesar Geronimo, and Griffey could play regularly. That was a Pete Rose trait. He'd do anything for the good of the team.

Things began going a little sour for the Reds in '77. The pitching staff, which had never been up to the ability of the hitters, was even more unstable, and injuries were making some of the veterans like Bench and Morgan miss valuable playing time. The Dodgers got off fast and swept to the division title. Even a mid-season acquisition of pitching star Tom Seaver was in vain. Pete had another good year, but the team didn't.

In '78 the Reds wanted to rebound. The team was still thin in the pitching department and soon found itself in a three-way race, not only with the Dodgers, but with the San Francisco Giants as well. The Giants were on top in the early going because they were playing the steadiest ball, while the Dodgers and Reds took turns going on winning and losing streaks. Pretty soon injuries began hitting the Reds. Morgan was subpar with torn stomach muscles and probably shouldn't have been playing at all. Bench was showing more wear and tear from the years behind the plate and was no longer able to catch on a daily basis. Even the great Tom Seaver was having an off year.

Somehow the Reds hung on, but the team was no longer the overpowering force it had been in 1975 and '76. By mid-June the team was again struggling and so was Pete. He was in an infrequent batting slump, having had just five hits in his last forty-four at bats. His season's average was just .265, rock bottom for Pete. And, of course, as soon as any thirty-seven-year-old athlete goes into a slump, there are those who interpret it as the beginning of the end.

Then on June 14, Pete banged out two hits in four trips against Dave Roberts of the Chicago Cubs. In Cincy's next game on the 16th he had two more against the Cardinals. And the next night he had two more, giving him six hits in twelve trips. Perhaps the slump was over.

It sure looked that way. Pete was getting a hit or two a

game. On June 24, he hit in his ninth straight game and did it by getting four hits off Bob Welch of the Dodgers. On June 30, he hit in his 15th straight and on July 4, made it 20 in a row against J. R. Richard of Houston. Now people began talking. Once a streak reaches 20 or so it begins to attract attention. And the fact that the team was back in the pennant race drew even more attention to Cincinnati and to Pete.

And Pete himself was getting pumped up. No one loves to play the game more than Charlie Hustle, and when he has added incentive, such as a pennant race and a hitting streak, he becomes almost superhuman. He kept hitting.

On July 9, he made it 25 with three hits against the Giants. His batting average was coming up now, also, moving through the .280s and back toward .300, where Pete always feels he belongs. On July 17, he went one for four against Stan Bahnsen of Montreal. The streak had reached 30 games.

Now everyone was watching him. In the long annals of baseball history, going back to pre-1900 days, there had been only 23 hitting streaks of 30 games or longer. Pete's was the 24th. The first mark he would be shooting at now would be Tommy Holmes's modern National League record of 37, set back in 1945.

In game number 32 there was a scare. Pete was hitless against the Phillies and up for perhaps the last time. With big Ron Reed on the mound Pete placed a perfect bunt down the third-base line and beat it out for a base hit. The next game his only hit was a leg job as he barely beat the throw of second-baseman Ted Sizemore, who had made a great play. He was to bunt against the Phillies again in game 41 to preserve the streak, prompting Phils third-baseman Mike Schmidt to say,

"Pete gave me two chances to stop the streak and I didn't do it either time. He's never bunted on me before, and then he laid down two perfect ones that I couldn't come up with. I've really got to respect him. He's the epitome of concentration. He's turned into my idol."

Pete follows through as another of his more than 3,000 hits sails into the outfield. *(Cincinnati Reds)*

Four times in all during the streak Pete saved himself with bunts, a tribute to his all-around skills. But more often than not he was stinging the ball, hitting sharp singles and doubles. Even many of his outs were on hard hit balls. On July 23, Pete rapped out two hits against Montreal to extend his hitting streak to 36 games. Now the Reds traveled to New York where Pete would have a chance to catch and pass Tommy Holmes.

It was ironic that the big games would be played in New York. Pete was always the enemy at Shea Stadium, especially since his 1973 playoff fight with then Mets shortstop Bud Harrelson. After that, the Shea patrons always vented a special wrath upon him. What's more, Tommy Holmes, the man whose record he was after, was an employee of the Mets, working in their community-relations department. So he would be on hand during the series.

Ex-Red Pat Zachry was on the mound in the 37th game, and a large crowd was there, too. No longer was Pete the enemy. Now they cheered his every move wildly, the past forgotten, only deep appreciation for a great ballplayer remained. As one writer put it, they seemed to realize they were seeing a very special ballplayer who, at age thirty-seven would not be around forever.

First time up against Zachry he flied out. Next time up same thing. Each time he went back to the dugout and waited patiently, taking his position at third when the Reds were in the field. He was playing with his usual intensity, but didn't seem to be pressing extra hard or to be uptight. Then when he grounded into a fielder's choice his third time up everyone began worrying.

His fourth at bat came in the seventh inning. Whether he liked it or not the pressure was on. Batting left-handed against Zachry Pete worked the count to 1-1. Then Zachry tried to change on the outside corner. Pete swung and sent a line drive to left. It dropped in front of left-fielder Steve Henderson, base hit. Pete had tied Holmes's record, and the crowd roared. He added another hit in the ninth and the crowd cheered him again, chanting his name over and over again.

"I couldn't believe the chant," Pete said. "I knew the New York fans were great, but I couldn't believe it. I wish I could have called time and shaken their hands."

Reds' Manager Sparky Anderson said that Pete loved the pressure.

"It's a great moment for him," said Sparky. "He loves the World Series, the playoffs, the All-Star Game, the attention. He lives for this."

Rose agreed. "I like pressure situations," he admitted. "They're fun. When people are urging me on, I can do things that are impossible sometimes."

The next night Pete was back again, this time facing the Mets' Craig Swan. His first time up, Pete flied out. Then he came up again in the third inning. He picked out a Swan fastball and slammed a liner past short into left. He had hit in his 38th straight game, a new modern National League record. The crowd gave Pete a standing ovation. Tommy Holmes came out on the field to give Pete the ball as the photogs snapped away. Pete loved every minute of it.

Even though the Reds lost the game, Pete got two more hits that night. Then after the game he was surrounded by reporters and newsmen, all asking about the streak, how far he could go, and reminding him of the men ahead of him. They were mostly great names. Ty Cobb had hit in 40 straight, George Sisler in 41. Then there was a player named Bill Dah-

The great Joe DiMaggio hit in 56 straight in 1941. Pete Rose challenged that mark in 1978. *(New York Yankees)*

len who had hit in 42 back in 1894. Willie Keeler had his 44 in 1897, and DiMaggio was on top with his incredible 56 in 1941.

"I feel like I know Cobb," Pete said. "I heard a lot about him early in my career from Waite Hoyt, who played against him, and I'm reading his biography now. I think we're a lot alike. He was small, tough, and liked to fight."

He was also determined to catch Keeler. "I'm a National Leaguer and so was Keeler," Pete said. "What difference does it make that he played before 1900 or after 1900?"

As for DiMaggio, Pete again sounded confident. "I told you guys I was hitting the ball good and I'll tell you one thing. I'm just starting now. I've got half the house built so now I've got to go on and build the rest."

Only Sparky Anderson sounded a warning. "I don't think anyone can catch DiMag," said the manager. "Too many things can go wrong. Seeing Pete break the National League record is the biggest thrill I've had as a manager, but fifty-six is an impossibility."

But Pete wasn't about to quit. By now the whole country was watching him. Programs were interrupted when Pete came to bat. Fans watching their local teams waited for the cameras to switch to the Cincinnati game so they could see Rose hit. The next night Pete was facing the Mets' Nino Espinosa.

First time up he grounded hard to shortstop. Next time up walked on four pitches as the crowd booed. Then he came up in the fifth inning. He tried a bunt, but it went foul. The next two pitches were balls. Then he fouled off three straight pitches. Espinosa threw another fastball and Pete swung, putting it deep into right center where it bounced past the Mets fielders and hit the wall. Pete pulled into second with a double. He had hit in 39 straight.

Now the Reds were off to Philadelphia where they'd be playing the Phils a doubleheader. In the first game Pete went out in the first. But facing righty Barry Lerch in the third, he stroked a double to the center to tie him with Cobb at 40. And in the second game he hit two hard shots for outs. Then in the sixth inning he laid down a perfect bunt in front of Schmidt for a hit. He was even with Sisler at 41. The tension continued to build.

Pete took care of the tension the next night. He rapped out three hits against Jim Lonborg and Jim Kaat to make it 42 straight. There was one more game against the Phillies. Facing lefty Larry Christenson, Pete flied out and grounded out his first two times. Then batting in fifth inning, he slammed a sharp single to left. The streak was up to 43. Asked again about DiMaggio's 56 games, Pete kidded the newsmen.

"Right now, I'm going after Sidney Stonestreet's forty-eight streak," he quipped. "You probably never heard of him. I can understand that . . . since I just made him up!"

So the team moved on to Atlanta for a July 31 game against the Braves. Veteran knuckleballer Phil Niekro was on the mound and he was always tough to hit. He got Pete twice, but in the sixth inning Pete lashed another single to tie Keeler's mark at 44 games. Now only DiMaggio lay ahead. Pete was generating an excitement that baseball hadn't seen in years.

The next night the Braves started a rookie left-hander named Larry McWilliams. He hadn't been with the team long, but had looked good. Many people thought Pete shouldn't have trouble wlth a rookie, but on the other hand, he had never seen McWilliams pitch before and might need an at bat or two to adjust.

In the first inning, Pete worked the count full at 3-2, then walked. He came up again in the second, the crowd screaming his name. Pete was sky high. He picked out the first pitch and lashed a hard liner back through the box. It looked like a sure hit. McWilliams, following through, stuck out his glove almost automatically, and the ball went right into it, ankle high. It was a great play, but in a sense a lucky one. Pete had been robbed of a hit.

Pete came up again in the fifth. He hit the ball hard again, but on a hop to the shortstop. He was thrown out. Relief-ace Gene Garber was on the mound when Pete came up in the seventh. Again Pete hit the ball hard, a line drive. But third-baseman Bob Horner caught the ball and turned it into a double play. Pete's luck seemed to be changing. Would he get another chance?

He did, facing Garber once again in the ninth. Pete tried a bunt on the first pitch, but it rolled foul. Now the pressure was on as never before. Garber has a herky-jerky motion and is very hard to hit. Pete watched the next two pitches go by for balls. Then he fouled the next. The count was 2-2. Garber threw a change on the outside corner. Pete swung . . . and missed. He was out, the streak was over at 44 games!

After the game Pete was still talking like the competitive player he is.

"No, I'm not relieved that it's over," he snapped. "I'm teed off. I wish it could go on forever. It's been exciting. I really enjoyed all of it."

So it was over. But it still lasted 44 games, drawing Pete even with Willie Keeler for the second longest hitting streak in baseball history. Pete had 70 hits in 182 trips for a .385 average during the streak. He raised his own average from .265 to .316. Perhaps it was symbolic that the Reds lost the game that the streak ended, 16-4. For after that, they never made a serious run for the division title. The Dodgers took it again.

But no one will forget the streak for a long time. For one thing, Pete will be around for a while yet. He had another .300 season with 198 hits. At age thirty-seven, he's still a great player. And since he got his 3,000th hit early in the year, his next goal is to pass Stan Musial as the all-time National League hit leader. Musial retired with 3,630.

As for another streak, it's hardly likely. But if you ask Pete, he'd probably say, why not. That's the kind of player he is. Every day is a new day, and a great day for baseball. In 1978, Pete Rose made it a great day for everyone.

Muhammad and the Olympians

IT CAN BE summed up in one sentence. Muhammad Ali has been the dominant force in the sport of boxing for nearly two decades. It all started when he was known as Cassius Clay and won the light-heavyweight title at the 1960 Rome Olympics and carried over to 1978 when he captured the heavyweight championship of the world for an unprecedented third time.

Between those two events so much has happened in the career of this complex man. He has been like a cat with nine lives, written off as both a person and a fighter, but he has climbed back to the top in both areas.

There have been so many highlights to Muhammad Ali's career that it would take an entire book to talk about all of them. However, one event does stand out, because it seemed like the one thing not even the great Ali could do. It was in November of 1974, when he captured the heavyweight title for the second time, defeating a mountain of a man named George Foreman.

Boxing has undergone something of a resurgence in the mid and late 1970s. Muhammad Ali certainly has had a great deal to do with it. But there was another event that captured the fancy of fight fans the world over. That was the unexpected triumph of five American fighters at the 1976 Olympics. So now let us look at these two diverse boxing events in the 1970s.

Muhammad Ali burst upon the scene at the 1960 Olympics. He was known as Cassius Clay then, a smiling, happy youngster of eighteen with great boxing skills. He danced and jabbed his way around the ring defeating older, more experienced fighters. When he won the gold medal he said it was his greatest thrill and he was going to sleep with it around his neck.

In October of that year he turned pro, winning his first fight against a heavyweight named Tunny Hunsaker in his hometown of Louisville, Kentucky. Fighting mostly in Louisville and Miami, young Cassius Clay won ten straight fights over the next fifteen months while he grew into a bona fide heavyweight and refined his skills.

In February of 1962 he had his first bout in Madison Square Garden, knocking out a good heavyweight named Sonny Banks in four rounds. The world began to know about Cassius Clay once more. At this time he also began working on his "act," his bragging, his predicting the round in which opponents would fall. He was on his way to becoming the self-proclaimed greatest, and perhaps the best public-relations man the fight game has ever had.

By February of 1964 he was ready for a shot at the title, still undefeated, and taking on Charles "Sonny" Liston, a bear of a man, huge and mean, who had taken the title from popular Floyd Patterson by destroying him in one round. In a rematch, Liston had done it again. He was so devastating that it seemed no man could beat him, let alone a twenty-two-year-old kid named Clay.

But Cassius predicted victory and he pulled it off. Showing

more speed of foot and hand than any heavyweight in many years, he danced and jabbed his way to a seventh-round TKO when Liston, overconfident and out of shape, couldn't continue. A wild Cassius danced around the ring in jubilation. He was heavyweight champion of the world at age twenty-two, the second-youngest man in history to hold the title (Patterson was the youngest).

But shortly after the bout Cassius Clay's life took a new twist. It was the mid-1960s, a time of change in the United States. There were many protest movements and much political unrest. Black people were looking for new freedoms that should have been theirs years earlier. Different groups were formed, and Cassius Clay suddenly announced he had become a Black Muslim, a group that followed the religion of Islam and at that time was for a separate black society apart from whites. Many people also felt the Black Muslims were militant and dangerous, though the Muslims maintained they only worried about self-defense.

At any rate, Cassius Clay discarded his name, which he said was his slave name, and became Muhammad Ali. He would continue fighting, of course, but now all his efforts would be directed toward helping the Muslims and working to achieve their goal. This immediately alienated many white people, and even some blacks. The Muslims at the time were looked upon with great suspicion and fear. So Muhammad Ali, well on his way to becoming one of the most popular athletes in America, suddenly did an about-face.

He did come back and knock Liston out in one round. Six months later he fought Floyd Patterson, the popular former champion. Ali ridiculed Patterson before the fight, then proceeded to administer a tortuous, taunting, twelve-round beating to the former champ before the fight was stopped.

By now, many former fans wanted Ali beaten. He kept saying over and over that he was the greatest of all time, the fastest, the prettiest, the best. Some were beginning to believe him. He had truly become a beautiful fighter to watch.

His speed of foot was amazing. He moved around the ring with the grace of a much smaller man, though he was well over two hundred pounds now, approaching two twenty. He could dance all night, changing directions in an instant, moving in and out so quickly that he couldn't be hit. Most fighters block punches with their hands and arms. Muhammad Ali was so quick that he just danced away or pulled his head back with his arms hanging at his side. No one could touch him.

There were no other really great heavyweights on the scene then, but Ali fought whoever was there and beat each one decisively. Then in 1967 he easily decisioned Ernie Terrell, who had been considered the National Boxing Association champion. That didn't mean much to most people, but it settled the title thing once and for all. Later in the year he knocked out veteran Zora Folley, his ninth defense of the title.

It was to be his last . . . for a while. The Vietnam war was still in progress then, and Muhammad Ali was drafted into the army. He refused to go, stating he was a minister of the Black Muslims and should be exempt. He was placed under arrest for refusing the draft. The boxing people immediately seized the opportunity to get the unpopular champ. They stripped him of the title. He was champion no longer.

Muhammad Ali never went to jail. He continued to appeal his case and it was finally dismissed. But he didn't fight for three years, three peak years in which he could have refined his skills even more. Finally, in October of 1970, he was given a license to fight again. He was now twenty-eight years old and the question was could he regain his skills after three years away.

He looked good in his comeback fight against Jerry Quarry, knocking the good heavyweight out in three rounds. Five months later he was fighting for the title again. Only this time he was up against Joe Frazier, a devastating left-hooker and old-fashioned brawler who had become champ in Muhammad's absence. Frazier came straight ahead, wasn't hard to hit, but rarely let his opponents rest. Both fighters were unbeaten when they met on March 8, 1971.

It was one of the greatest fights of all time. The two men went at it for fifteen rounds, nonstop, Frazier boring in and catching Ali with shots to the body and head, Muhammad in turn peppering Frazier with rights and lefts to the head. The two fighters taunted each other, and Muhammad played to the crowd. At one point Frazier simply dropped his gloves and let Muhammad hit him five straight times in the face. Then he laughed. That's the kind of fight it was.

In the fourteenth round, Frazier sent Muhammad to the canvas with a tremendous left hook. Somehow Muhammad got up and finished the fight, but Frazier won a unanimous decision. He was still champion and Muhammad Ali had lost the first fight of his career.

Despite the loss, a strange thing was happening. The furor of Vietnam was fading into history, and although Muhammad was still a Muslim, the group had modified its policies toward whites and was no longer as feared. At the same time, Muhammad began appearing more and more on television talk shows and in public. His wondrous personality was again winning over his former fans. He still called himself the greatest and was known all over the world. He was once again one of the most popular athletes anywhere.

But he had to keep fighting. In March of 1973 he lost his second fight, a decision to tough Ken Norton, who broke Muhammad's jaw during an exchange. It was obvious to everyone now that the three-year layoff had taken its toll. Muhammad was no longer the dancing master, able to escape punches as easily as he pleased. He couldn't move for as long and couldn't escape as many punches. The old Ali would have beaten Norton easily.

Yet they fought again in September and Ali won a close twelve-round decision. Things had changed by then. In January of that year Frazier had lost his title to big George Foreman, a ponderous plodder with a devastating punch. Joe's style, which made him so easy to hit, spelled doom as Foreman's big punches took him out in two rounds.

Now Muhammad wanted Foreman. But first he fought

Frazier again, a twelve-rounder that was almost as tough as the first one. This time Muhammad won the decision and signed to meet Foreman in October of 1974 for the championship. The fight would be held in the African country of Zaire.

To most people, this was the fight Muhammad Ali could not win. Foreman, like Liston years back, looked unbeatable. He was so big and he punched so hard. And Ali was not the fighter he had been. That was obvious. Plus he was now thirty-two years old. There were people who actually felt sorry for Muhammad just thinking about what might happen. After destroying Frazier, Foreman had also destroyed Ken Norton in two rounds, the same Norton who had beaten Ali once and fought him tough a second time.

Veteran fight manager Gil Clancy kind of summed up everyone's feelings when he said, "If Muhammad has any ace in the hole at all, and I don't think he does, and if there is any way he can win this fight, and I doubt that there is, then the key is Zaire. He will turn the entire arena against the other guy." That was true, for by then Muhammad might have been the most popular athlete in the world.

But still, the odds were high. Eddie Futch, who trained and managed Joe Frazier, said this. "I don't care what the scorecards say because Ali has to be erect after 15 for the scorecards to count, and there is no way he will be. He isn't strong enough. Strength on strength, he can't handle George."

Only Angelo Dundee, Muhammad's veteran trainer, said it differently. "My guy will knock him out midway in the fight," said Dundee, and everyone laughed.

They figured Muhammad would try to turn back the clock and dance, keeping away from Foreman, but the time would come when he'd have to come down off the bicycle and Foreman would catch him. As Dick Sadler, Foreman's manager, put it:

"When George hits a guy he lifts him off his feet. To win, Ali must have some sort of a break, a fluke. There's too much against him."

Finally it was fight night. In all the years of the heavy-weight division only one fighter, Floyd Patterson, had lost and then regained the title. Muhammad Ali wanted to be the second.

The bell rang for round one and the audience held their breaths. Literally the whole world was watching as the fight was beamed around the globe on closed-circuit TV and by other means. People expected Ali to come out dancing and jabbing. But he didn't. He took a few steps into the center of the ring, then backed into a corner and covered up. Maybe he was terrified of Foreman's fists? No one could figure it out.

Even Ali's corner people were yelling at him. So he moved out of the corner and onto the ropes, where he covered up again. On the ropes he alternated covering up and leaning back. Foreman began to throw his heavy punches, but Ali was picking them off or leaning out of the way. Just before the end of the round Ali came off the ropes and suddenly hit Foreman with a series of quick, short punches in the face. The crowd roared, and Foreman looked puzzled and angry.

Ali's cornermen continued to tell him to dance and move. But the former champ had devised his own game plan. "I know what I'm doing," he said. And in the second and third rounds he continued to lie on the ropes, a maneuver he later called the Rope-a-Dope. Foreman kept pressuring and punching, but his punches were doing little, if any, damage. He couldn't figure out a way to get through Ali's defense, or whatever you'd call it. And he was wasting his energy. Most of Foreman's fights had ended so quickly that there was some question about his stamina.

Late in the third round, Ali came off the ropes to hit Foreman with another combination of shots, and some thought they saw Foreman stagger slightly. Could Ali's plan be working? In his corner Ali said Foreman's punches weren't that bad and that he'd continue to catch them on his arms and shoulders.

In the fourth Ali started another of his tactics. He began

talking to Foreman, taunting him, while the big man continued to pound away at the man on the ropes. He was saying things like "Is that the best you can do?" "You can't punch, show me something." "That's a sissy punch."

Soon it was obvious that Foreman was tiring badly. His punches were slower and lacked any snap. He began to get tangled in his own feet increasingly, while Ali did not seem any the worse for wear. Finally ringsiders heard Ali say to Foreman, "Now it's my turn."

He started coming off the ropes and throwing punches, combinations and right-hand leads, all of which were finding their mark. By the eighth round Foreman looked out on his feet. The crowd of people watching couldn't believe it. Ali stalked the big man and sent him to the canvas with a series of lefts and rights. Foreman tried to get up, but couldn't. He had nothing left. The fight was over. Muhammad Ali had regained the heavyweight championship of the world in one of the great upsets in sports history.

Of course, the Muhammad Ali saga has continued from there. Foreman never got another shot at the title and eventually faded from the scene. Ali kept on. He gave Frazier another shot thinking Joe was about through, but the "Thrilla in Manila" turned out to be another grueling, exhausting fight. At one point Ali thought he would have to quit, but his great fighting heart took him on and it was Smokin' Joe who finally packed it in after fourteen rounds.

"It was the closest thing to death," said an exhausted Ali.

Then there were controversial decisions against Jimmy Young and Norton again. Ali was being hit more, though still unmarked, and many urged him to retire. But some said that he couldn't because the title was his stage and Ali the showman needed the attention.

In February of 1978 Ali fought Leon Spinks, who had won the 1976 Olympic light-heavyweight title. Spinks had just seven pro fights and Ali took him lightly. But Leon had youth and stamina, and won the fight against an old, slow

Muhammad Ali sends George Foreman reeling from a hard right to the head in the seventh round of their championship bout as referee Zack Clayton looks on. Ali knocked Foreman out in the eighth round to regain the heavyweight title. *(Wide World Photo)*

Ali. Then there was a rematch in September, and Ali, fighting for his life, defeated Spinks to win the title for a third time.

Again people are urging him to retire, but at age thirty-six, Ali may go on if the price is right and he feels he can do it. He has earned millions of dollars and the respect of millions of people. His career has had many, many highlights and there have been many memorable fights.

But the one time he really beat the odds was in Zaire against Foreman. Very few people thought he could win. But Ali used his great boxing mind and his diminishing skills to perfection and did it. And it had to be one of the great sports events of the seventies.

The other event that helped the resurgence of boxing in the 1970s was the Olympic Games of 1976 in Montreal, Canada. United States boxers traditionally have not done all that well in Olympic competition. More often than not, the veteran European fighters or fighters from the Far East do better.

After all, it's amateur competition, and the United States fighters are usually very young, mostly teenagers, and vastly inexperienced, at the beginning of their careers. If they're older they've undoubtedly already turned pro and are not eligible for the Olympics.

European fighters, by contrast, are usually much older and tremendously experienced. They've been fighting as amateurs for years and are toughened veterans, especially those from the Communist-block countries where the government subsidizes the athletes. The fighters can remain amateurs as long as they choose, the government giving them jobs and allowing them to train adequately.

The United States has had some great Olympic champions, usually in the higher weight classes. Floyd Patterson won the middleweight title in the '52 Games. Cassius Clay did it in 1960. Joe Frazier was Olympic heavyweight king in 1964 and George Foreman in 1968.

Going into the '76 Games, the U.S. team was again an unknown quantity. The coaches were Pat Nappi, an Italian-American from Syracuse, New York, and Tom Johnson, a black man from Indianapolis. The team was very close-knit, living and training together. And word was that there were some quality fighters there who could make a lot of noise.

The United States fighters were well skilled in boxing techniques, moved and jabbed, punched when they had to. Traditionally, the European fighters are slower, straight-ahead punchers who will take three shots to give one and wear their opponents down. The U.S. coaches hoped their fighters would be skillful enough to overcome these older, stronger men, some of whom were over thirty years old.

One team to fear was the Cubans. Since their great heavyweight, Teofilo Stevenson had knocked out American Duane Bobick in the '72 Games, the Cubans had also been building a tough team, with skills similar to that of the Americans. As it turned out, the two teams dominated the Montreal fight scene.

"We knew what we were up against," said Pat Nappi, "maturity and experience. Our kids would be outexperienced 10 to 1. When a man becomes a champion in an Iron Curtain country you can bet he's good. Look at Russia, the last time I was there in 1971 they had 480,000 amateur fighters. We had 10,000. But we knew how to beat that advantage and how to beat their styles.

"What they do best is drive straight ahead, pressing our kids into a corner or against the ropes and then using their maturity on them. Our kids were never experienced enough to stay in there very long against that."

So the American fighters were taught to move forward

This is the great 1976 U.S. Olympic Boxing Team which took home seven medals. In front, left to right, Coach Pet Nappi and Assistant Coach Tom Johnson. Standing, left to right, heavyweight John Tate (bronze medal), light heavyweight Leon Spinks (gold medal), middleweight Michael Spinks (gold medal), light middleweight Charles Walker, welterweight Clinton Jackson, light welterweight "Sugar" Ray Leonard (gold medal), lightweight Howard Davis (gold medal), featherweight Davey Armstrong, bantamweight Charles Mooney (silver medal), flyweight Leo Randolph (gold medal), and light flyweight Louis Curtis. *(Photo courtesy Larry Breeden)*

with powerful jabs followed by combinations, to force the other fighters backward. When the U.S. fighters did have to retreat, they were taught to go to the right or left, never straight back. After that, it was a matter of getting the fighters into superb condition and give them as much experience as possible.

"Our kids gave us everything they had," said Nappi. "We couldn't ask for more."

In Montreal, both the Eastern Europeans and Cubans didn't think all that much of the U.S. team. They figured the U.S. had another second-rate entry. But in the early fights a distinct pattern began emerging. The U.S. fighters were good, very good. They had a chance for seven or eight medals. And as they went along, their personalities emerged. It was a diverse, interesting, and highly skilled group of fighters.

The first American fighter to make it to the finals was little Leo Randolph, a flyweight from Tacoma, Washington, and still in high school. He was a quiet youngster, and deeply religious. He went up against Cuban Ramon Duvalon, in the first confrontation between the two countries.

Randolph danced and jabbed, and more often than not beat the Cuban to the punch in a close fight. It was a split vote, but Randolph won the first gold medal for the American team by a 3-2 vote.

"This is the greatest thing that has happened to me since I turned Christian in 1962," he said.

Next came Charles Mooney, an Army sergeant, fighting for the bantamweight crown. Mooney had a bad cold in the final and was beaten by a North Korean, 5-0. He took a silver medal.

After that came Howard Davis, Jr., a twenty-year-old lightweight from Glen Cove, New York. Davis was perhaps the most highly polished of the American fighters. His style is reminiscent of early Muhammad Ali, as he dances around slipping punches and delivering his in sharp, fast combinations.

"I'm no brawler," Davis said. "The Europeans take a lot of punches, get cut up, and look ugly. It's part of their day's work. But I don't want that. I'm not crazy."

But he was good. His mother had died just before the Olympics and Howard dedicated his fights to her. In the final he fought a Romanian, Simion Cutov, a two-time European champion and veteran of more than two hundred bouts. Davis made it look easy. He outspeeded, outdanced, and outpunched the Romanian in a superb display of boxing skills. He won the gold medal with a 5-0 decision and looked like the best amateur lightweight in the world.

Next up was light-welterweight Sugar Ray Leonard, perhaps the most charismatic of the U.S. fighters. Like Davis, he was lightning fast, but he enjoyed mixing it up a bit more and often threw furious flurries of punches which brought the crowd to its feet time and again. He had very sore, swollen hands from his previous fights, but before the final, he said,

"One more fight, then it's over. I've been fighting here with one hand. Now I'll let go with everything. What do I have to lose."

He'd be up against a tough one, southpaw Andras Aldama of Cuba, a devastating puncher who had hit a Bulgarian so hard they thought the man's neck was broken.

Sugar Ray came out circling his opponent, going to work with both hands. He never gave Aldama a chance to set himself and throw his explosive left. In the second round he dropped Aldama with a flurry before the bell. Then in the third round he let it all out as promised, punching faster than the eye could see, banging Aldama with a hook and a succession of rights. The Cuban was holding on at the bell and Sugar Ray took the gold with a 5-0 decision.

Next came the fighting Spinks brothers from St. Louis. Michael was a middleweight and Leon a light heavyweight. Both were power fighters, unlike Davis and Leonard, but they knew how to punch, didn't just swing wildly.

Michael went to the final against a twenty-seven-year-old Russian, who was some seven years older than the American. But Michael quickly moved inside in the first round and peppered the Russian with rights and lefts. In the second round he floored the older man with a looping right and was working him over in the corner when the round ended.

The third round was more of the same. Spinks was taking him apart with devastating precision. At 1:54 of the round a left hook to the midsection doubled the Russian over. He tried to claim a foul but the ref said no. He had just been badly beaten and Michael Spinks had taken America's fourth gold medal.

Next it was twenty-three-year-old Leon. He was already overjoyed by his brother's win, saying, "I wanted him to win more than I wanted me to win. I kept asking the Lord to watch over him."

Leon would not have it easy. He'd be up against a powerful Cuban, twenty-two-year-old Sixto Soria, a fighter with a devastating right and the favorite. This was to be the most grueling fight of the Olympics.

Both men came out punching. Neither would back off or give an inch. The Cuban was a bit faster, but Spinks seemed to hit harder. Near the end of the round Leon staggered Soria with a right, hit him with a second, then dropped him to the canvas with a third. In the second round Soria seemed to be coming hack, hitting Leon several good shots, but Spinks's strength and heart turned it around and he battered the Cuban once more.

Early in the third Spinks caught Soria again, with a big right. It spun him around and Leon chased him across the ring. Another right put the Cuban down. He got up, but was unable to continue. Leon Spinks had won the United States' fifth gold medal, and with brother Michael, had become the first brother act to win Olympic boxing titles.

Heavyweight John Tate gave the U.S. a seventh medal, a bronze. He was stopped by Teofilo Stevenson of Cuba in the semifinals. Stevenson went on to take his second Olympic heavyweight crown.

But the United States had surprised the world with five gold medals, a silver, and a bronze. The boxers had all shown superior skills and conditioning, and gave the sport a tremendous boost back home, especially at the amateur level.

At this writing, all the medal winners except Mooney have turned professional. Three men, Davis, Leonard, and John Tate are unbeaten and being brought along slowly. Experts feel Davis and Leonard have a fine chance to become champions. It's too early to tell with Randolph and Tate.

Michael Spinks is also unbeaten, but his career has taken a turn since his brother's two fights with Muhammad Ali. Michael hasn't fought in a while, and his future must now be considered in doubt.

By now everyone knows about Leon. He fought seven times (six wins and a draw) and then upset Ali to become heavyweight champion, only to lose it to Ali some seven months later. He's had personal problems and problems with the people handling him, so his future, too, must now be considered doubtful.

But no matter what happens to all these men, no one will forget the excitement they caused at the 1976 Olympics, when they brought United States amateur boxing back to the top in a blaze of gold and glory.

The Triumph
of Nadia

THE GREATEST possible achievement for an amateur athlete is to win a gold medal at the Olympic Games. Thousands upon thousands of young athletes all over the world practice for years for a chance at Olympic glory. But only a small percentage of them are good enough to go to the Games, which are held once every four years. And of these, a still smaller percentage wind up winners.

Some can use their gold medals and their fame to go on to other careers. Some move on to professional sports where they can make big money with their skills and talents. Still others return to their homelands and are soon largely forgotten. It depends on the athlete and the sport.

But every once in a while an Olympic athlete comes along who captures the imagination of the whole world. And at the same time, this athlete becomes a barometer that changes the flow of his or her particular sport.

Nadia Comaneci was such an athlete. In 1976, Nadia was

a fourteen-year-old gymnast from Romania who captivated the crowds at the Olympics in Montreal, Canada. Not only did she demonstrate a poise and style beyond her years, but her daring expertise in all facets of gymnastics helped revolutionize the sport and won her three gold medals along the way. She received worldwide acclaim for her great Olympic feat, and was instrumental in starting a gymnastics boom in the United States and in other countries of the world.

There was a time when gymnasts had to be at least eighteen years old to be in the Olympics. But with so many young people in the sport, the age was dropped to fourteen. In came Nadia Comaneci at age fourteen and showed she was the best female gymnast in the world. She could turn, twist, flip, swing, leap, and maneuver her eighty-six pound body in a way no one else could. And she was doing things that only older gymnasts and mostly men had done before. In fact, she was even doing things that no one—man or woman—had ever done before.

The success of Nadia Comaneci and some other young gymnasts changed the thinking of many longtime gymnastics coaches. They realized that youngsters of ten, twelve, and

A very serious Nadia waits for her chance to compete.
(International Gymnast)

fourteen could learn the difficult maneuvers very early, that they had tremendous control of their small, lithe bodies. And most importantly, perhaps, was the fact that at that age they are willing to try almost anything, because they have little or no fear.

This is not to say that youngsters are taken advantage of and pushed to perform the impossible. If they are brought along carefully, by good, competent, caring coaches, they can learn the difficult things early, perfect them, and have a better chance of reaching their full potential than if they had waited until they were say, sixteen, to begin.

Take the case of Nadia Comaneci. She was born on November 11, 1961, in Onesti, Romania, a city of about 40,000 people set in the foothills of the Carpathian Mountains. Nadia's father was an auto mechanic, her mother an office worker. There is one other child in the family, a boy four years younger than Nadia.

Romania is an Eastern European country, one of the countries where the government is very much involved in athletics, paying for the discovery, training, and participation of young athletes. So the best athletes become involved in amateur sports. This doesn't always work the same way in the United States, where amateur athletes in certain sports must work and train on their own. And others become professionals as soon as they can to earn money.

In Eastern countries including Russia, for example, top amateur athletes often live nearly as well as professional athletes here. Perhaps it isn't exactly fair, but that's the way it is. And this is also not to say that they don't care about the athletes themselves in Eastern Europe. In most cases, they do.

Nadia Comaneci is a perfect example. She was a happy youngster in her very early years. She had a comfortable home and many friends. Like the youngsters in America, she started school when she was five years old. When she was six, a man named Bela Karolyi came to her school. He was a gymnastics coach who fell in love with the sport after he met his wife, Marta, who was a gymnast.

Bela Karolyi came to Nadia's school to look for young

children who seemed to be good at gymnastics or who wanted to try the sport. He was on the playground when he saw two young girls playing.

"They were running and jumping and pretending to be gymnasts," he remembers. "But before I could approach them the bell rang and they joined the crowd of children all rushing inside. I lost sight of them. So I started going into all the classes looking for them. I had no luck. Suddenly all the little girls were looking alike. I went around a second time and still couldn't find them. The third time I started asking a question in each class. I asked, "Who loves gymnastics here? And in the third class two girls jumped up, shouting, 'We do!' I had found them."

One girl has since gone on to become a promising ballet dancer in Romania. The other was Nadia. Bela Karolyi talked to both young girls and after school took them over to the gymnasium for a test.

"We have a very simple test," the coach said. "We ask the youngsters to run a fifteen-meter sprint, make a long jump, and then walk across the balance beam. If they are afraid of the beam we just send them home immediately."

The balance beam is used in gymnastics competition and is just four inches wide. The first time she got up on it, Nadia walked right across it, as if she were strolling down the street. Karolyi knew he had a girl with great potential and he soon began working with her. That was easy, because Nadia loved gymnastics, loved to practice, and learned fast.

She soon settled into a routine. After school, she took a long nap, then went over to the gym for three or four hours of practice. She also gave up many of the junk foods her friends ate, like candy and other sweets. So from age six, she was training like an athlete.

When she was just seven, her coach entered her in her first competition. It was the Romanian Junior Championships and Nadia finished thirteenth. That wasn't bad, considering she was the youngest gymnast there and had only been working at it for a year.

To say she improved rapidly would be an understatement.

For one year later, at age eight, she went back to the same meet and won it! She became the Romanian Junior Champion. Now it was obvious that her potential was unlimited.

Yet as the months and years passed, and Nadia won more championships, she never lost her love for the sport. Many people, especially in the West, feel that Eastern European athletes are not really happy working at their sports, that they are almost forced to do it. But just watching Nadia you could see this was not so. And she sometimes talked about it.

"Of course it is more work now than it used to be," she said. There was a time when it was all fun. But I don't feel I have lost my childhood or anything like that. And I still practice with much pleasure."

A large part of the reason for that was Bela Karolyi and his wife. They were very concerned about their young athletes and watched over them carefully.

"We feel it is emotionally easier for a young person to bear success than for an adult," said Bela Karolyi. "But it is still very important for me and my wife to occupy ourselves with Nadia. It is up to us and her parents to see that she remains what she is, a normal girl of her age. She is well aware that she is first of all a schoolgirl and a member of our team, and each time we go abroad, her only concern is to come back to her family as soon as possible."

Nadia got better and better. She was learning and mastering all phases of gymnastics. She worked on the uneven bars, which are two wooden bars set apart off the ground at different heights. Gymnasts swing and loop around them, do handstands on them, going from one maneuver to another very quickly. When they dismount they usually flip or somersault through the air and land on their feet.

The balance beam, as mentioned before, is just four inches wide and quite long. A gymnast will dance, jump, turn, do flips and handstands on it. Done well, the balance beam can be a beautiful exercise.

Floor exercises are done on a mat without any equipment. The gymnast makes up her own program, which is done to music. In some ways it's almost like a dance, with a combination of tumbling exercises, flips, somersaults, and cartwheels. Then there is vaulting competition in which the gymnast does a series of flips in midair.

Nadia practiced all these things constantly. By the time she was thirteen she was almost five feet tall and weighed about eighty-six pounds. She had to be careful not to gain any more weight unless she grew taller. That was the right weight for her size. In early 1975, Coach Karolyi decided to let Nadia compete in the European Championships. It was her first senior competition. She would be going up against some of the best gymnasts in the world.

During the floor exercises, Nadia showed both charm and grace. *(International Gymnast)*

To the surprise of those who didn't know her, Nadia performed brilliantly. She was calm and confident. And when it was over, she had won. It was the beginning of a new wave in gymnastics. Two other teenagers finished behind her, while Russia's Ludmilla Turischeva, at age twenty-three and a five-time world champion, finished fourth. The youngsters were coming, and Nadia was at the head of the class.

She then began traveling around the world with her team. She won every meet she was entered in, and in Canada had six perfect scores of 10. No gymnast had ever had more than one perfect 10 in a single meet before.

When she went to New York the people loved her. She was in the American Cup Meet where she competed against one girl from each of the eleven different countries. She won with little trouble. The people had all kinds of questions for her. She answered with the help of an interpreter and talked about her skills.

"I am so good because I work very hard for it," she said. "Gymnastics requires grace above all, but also courage, perseverance and hard work."

Most agreed with her. An American gymnastics official, Frank Bare, called her "a perfectionist who has no weak events," while her own coach, Bela Karolyi, said:

"Nadia is very serious. It's not her nature to smile much. But she is also never afraid and has never cried."

Finally it was time for the 1976 Olympic Games. The Russians once again had a very strong team. They had won most of the medals at the 1972 games. But the Romanian girls were also good, and many felt Nadia would take some of the gold from the Russians.

There were also many very young gymnasts at the Games in '76, teenagers who seemed much too young for international competition. But as Nadia proved, they weren't. Bela Karolyi also talked about the reasons there were so many young gymnasts.

"A gymnast's career should last from the age of eight to

Nadia flies through the air during a maneuver on the uneven bars.
(International Gymnast)

about twenty," he said. "During those years there is no fear and no real problem. Women gymnasts have done so many more difficult things in the last few years because they are younger now."

The first event Nadia was in was the uneven bars. A performance on the bars lasts just twenty-three seconds, because the gymnast performs many difficult maneuvers one right after another. It takes a tremendous amount of strength and energy and couldn't really last much longer.

Olympic judges are usually very tough. The competition is close and sometimes less than a point can separate two performers. But in the long history of gymnastics competition in the Olympics, no performer had ever received a perfect score of 10 for any one performance. Then Nadia Comaneci got on the uneven bars.

Her routine was breathtaking, as she deftly went from one

maneuver to another without faltering and with grace and self-assurance. All eyes were on her, and when the judges voted, a collective gasp came from the large crowd. Nadia had gotten a perfect 10, the first ever in Olympic gymnastics competition.

From a technical standpoint, her performance was incredible. Frank Bare of the U.S. made this comment:

"There is always the challenge inherent in gymnastics to do something that nobody has ever done before," he said. "Here we are at the Olympics and Nadia does something on the uneven bars—a piked front somersault in a straddle position from top bar back to top bar—that people had talked about before, but no one, man or woman, had ever tried it. And Nadia pulls it off like a piece of cake. That must be more exciting than getting a ten!"

Nadia herself was the picture of cool. Asked if she was surprised by the perfect score, she said,

"No, I wasn't surprised. I knew it was flawless. I have done it fifteen times before."

And Nadia wasn't finished. It seemed that everything she did was coming up 10's. She was beautiful to watch on the balance beam and was cute and pixielike during her floor exercises. The crowd followed her wherever she was, but she often seemed oblivious to them. She just kept concentrating on her sport.

When it was all over, Nadia had astounded the world. On seven occasions she had gotten a score of 10 from the judges. And she took home three gold medals, including best all-around gymnast, a silver team medal, and a bronze. Soon the whole world knew about the little Romanian gymnast.

Some people criticized the judges for giving Nadia so many 10's. "Nobody's perfect," was the cry heard more than once. But former United States gymnast Kathy Rigby Mason put it all in perspective.

"The judges were in a box," she said. "They started out

giving high scores, and Nadia was so superior to every girl there that they had no choice but to give her tens."

Then she added, "But don't take anything away from Nadia. If she were doing what she has been doing all alone in an empty room, I'd still have to say that she would get the tens."

Nadia herself said she was confident, adding, "I was sure I would win," and her coach, Bela Karolyi, sounded a warning to others.

"As far as I can tell, Nadia is still five years from her peak. I'm sure she'll get better and be back for the 1980 Olympics. Nadia has all the qualities. She has the physical qualities—strength, speed, and agility. And she has the mental qualities—intelligence and the power to concentrate. And above everything else, Nadia has courage."

Of course, no one knows what the future holds for anyone. As of late 1978, Nadia's performance had fallen off. She had grown and put on weight. Perhaps she must adjust to her new physical size before she can regain her 1976 form. Only time will tell.

But no matter what happens, people will remember the 1976 Olympic Games. There were many great performances in the Games that year. There always are. Yet when people think of the Montreal Olympiad, they think of Nadia Comaneci, the little Romanian gymnast who astounded everyone with her great skills and total command of her sport. At age fourteen, she was a great Olympic athlete in every sense of the word.

The Lakers
Reach the Top

IN THE 1960s, one team dominated the sport of professional basketball. They were the Boston Celtics, and their dominance began in the late fifties when center Bill Russell joined the team. Russell retired after a final championship in 1968-69, so as the decade turned, several teams looked to jump to the top. There would never be another dynasty such as the Celts, but there were some good teams in the NBA nevertheless.

When the smoke of the first post-Russell season had ended, the 1969-70 champions were the New York Knickerbockers. The Knicks had done it with an uncanny brand of team play and defense, led by a rugged center named Willis Reed, ball-hawking guard Walt Frazier, and power forward Dave DeBusschere. But it had truly been a team effort. In the final round of the playoffs that year, the Knicks had been extended to a full seven games before defeating the Los Angeles Lakers 113-99.

Ah, yes, the Lakers. Always a bridesmaid. . . . The team that couldn't win it all. The franchise had come to L.A. from Minneapolis in 1960-61. As the Minneapolis Lakers, the team dominated the league in the late 1940s and early 1950s, when big George Mikan, Jim Pollard, and Vern Mikkelsen were the bulwarks underneath. But since moving to L.A., the team just couldn't get past that final hurdle.

Just look at the record. In 1961-62, the Lakers reached the championship round of the playoffs before losing to the Celtics. They lost in overtime in the seventh game. How close can you get? But that was only the beginning of a decade of frustration.

On five more occasions in the 1960s, the Lakers reached the final round only to be turned back by the Russell-led Celtics each time. Then when Russell retired, along came the Knicks and they whipped L.A. in the finals. Between 1961-62 and 1969-70, the Lakers lost in the final round seven times. That could be a study in frustration unmatched in the history of sports.

During most of the 1960s, the Lakers were led by a pair of superstars, two of the greatest players ever to come into the NBA. They were forward Elgin Baylor and guard Jerry West. They'd get the team there, but never all the way there. Most people blamed it on the lack of a quality center to go head to head with Russell.

Then in 1968 the team made a trade. Coming to L.A. was Wilt Chamberlain, the 7 foot 1 inch giant considered by many as the most talented big man ever to play pro ball. But like the Lakers, Chamberlain was always a bridesmaid. Though he set all kinds of scoring and rebounding records from the time he came into the league in 1959-60, he nevertheless played in the shadow of Bill Russell.

To many, Russell was the team man, Chamberlain the individual. Russell would sacrifice, Chamberlain was selfish. Russell was a competitor, Chamberlain a quitter. Only once in the decade of the sixties did Chamberlain break through.

In 1966-67, his Philadelphia 76ers finally cracked through the Celtics and won it all. But they slipped back the next year. And whenever his team didn't win, Chamberlain always seemed to get the blame.

He came to L.A. in 1968-69 and right away people said the Lakers couldn't lose. After all, with Chamberlain joining Baylor and West, the Lakers now had three of the greatest players in the game.

The Lakers won their division easily that year and missed by two games of having the best record in the NBA. And all three superstars averaged more than twenty points a game. But in the playoffs the aging Celtics with that combination of teamwork, intensity, tradition, and pride prevailed. And when the Knicks took it the next year, there was really a lot of grumbling in Los Angeles.

In 1970-71, the Lakers were beaten in the Western Division finals by the eventual champions, the Milwaukee Bucks, an expansion team of a few years earlier, but one that featured the new supergiant of the game, Lew Alcindor (later known as Kareem Abdul-Jabbar) and the aging but still outstanding Oscar Robertson. Baylor was hurt all year, playing in just two games, and with the rise of the Bucks it began to look as if the Lakers might never get that elusive title, at least not without a complete rebuilding program.

At the beginning of the 1971-72 season some thought the team might collapse completely. Baylor was thirty-six and coming off surgery. West was also in his thirties, and Wilt was nearly thirty-five. Plus he had had knee surgery in 1969-70, and some said he wasn't the same player he used to be. Others pointed out the fact that Wilt was still the most physically imposing man in the whole sport, a true mountain of a man with tremendous strength. But then again, Chamberlain had always brought out a score of pros and cons among basketball fans.

There were a few basketball people who pointed out the fact that the Lakers still had a talented team. Wilt shouldn't have to worry about his offense. Defensively he was still tops,

Veteran center Wilt Chamberlain was the key to the Lakers' success. Here he dunks the ball despite efforts by Kareem Abdul-Jabbar (33) to stop him. *(Team Magazine)*

an intimidator, and the best rebounder in the game. West, though past thirty and injury prone, was still one of the best when healthy. Young Gail Goodrich looked ready to become another high-scoring guard. Harold "Happy" Hairston was a fine power forward and rebounder if his mood could match his nickname.

The problem was Baylor. Could he come back? Some thought the team would be better off without him. After all, Elgin, like many superstars, was hesitant to admit he had slipped, and his efforts to show he could still do it might hurt the team. Waiting in the wings was 6-5 Jim McMillian, an intelligent player from Columbia, who could shoot well, and more importantly, blend his talents to the rest of the team. The bench wasn't real strong, but perhaps the team could get by.

At the outset of the season the team was trying to feel its

way. Baylor was struggling and it was obvious, but the others were playing well, especially Goodrich, who was living up to his scoring potential. Hairston was also playing well, and Wilt and West both looked healthy and hungry. But something wasn't right. Then about nine games into the season, something happened to change everything.

Elgin Baylor suddenly announced his retirement. The man many think was the greatest ever at his position realized he could no longer do the job. Instead of just hanging on, he decided to pack it in. It was the right move, for Elgin and for the team. For when he quit, Jim McMillian became a starter and everything suddenly jelled.

McMillian provided the final link. His presence gave the team more movement, more fluidity, more cohesiveness. Baylor's presence had made the others uneasy. They felt Elg should get the ball and sometimes went out of their way to get it to him. It slowed the offense. McMillian just fit into the flow. When the shot was there, he took it, but made no demands. West and Goodrich were freed to do most of the big scoring. McMillian got his points when they came, and sometimes a lot of them came. Hairston was content to pick up underneath, play defense, and rebound.

And as for Wilt, he began doing the things that make a team work. He rebounded like a tiger, played defense, blocked shots, and intimidated opponents. He was no longer interested in scoring fifty points a game, something he had once done. He knew he could score. But he didn't have to with this team. When someone suggested he was a "new" Wilt Chamberlain, the big man bristled.

"New Wilt Chamberlain!" he barked. "I'm the same man I've always been, the only man who ever played this game and switched his style to suit his team. What I'm doing I've been doing for a couple of years now.

"The team is running more, so when I take down a defensive rebound I am passing out faster, but running has always been my favorite way of playing. People have always said that Wilt slows down a team, but I prefer the fast break."

Then he mentioned things that had bothered him so often in his great career.

"One man doesn't win or lose in this game. It's a team game. I got too much blame for losing, but I don't want too much credit for winning."

Wilt had also been named captain of the team when Baylor retired. On October 31, just a couple of weeks into the season, the Lakers faced the Baltimore Bullets. West was coming off a minor injury, McMillian was settling in as a starter, and the team was intact.

That night in L.A. the Lakers won handily. Wilt scored just 12 points, but grabbed 25 rebounds and handed off for 6 assists. On one play he had the crowd on its feet when he grabbed the ball right out of the hands of powerful Wes Unseld and fired the length of the court to Goodrich for a hoop. The game was never in doubt. What no one could have known then was that the Lakers were about to embark on the greatest winning streak in the history of professional sports.

The next night they won in Oakland with Wilt grabbing 19 rebounds, and the next night back in L.A. against the Knicks he had 20 rebounds and 7 assists. Two nights later in Chicago he had 20 rebounds and 8 assists. Then in Philadelphia he rebounded and intimidated, and the Lakers won by forty points. The team had won five in a row. No one was really thinking streak then, but when they continued to win, more and more people began to watch the Lakers.

Everyone was playing well. West and Goodrich were both averaging more than 25 a game. McMillian was around 18, Hairston 14, and Wilt 12. West was leading the league in assists, Wilt in rebounds. And people who had criticized Wilt for years suddenly realized that he was the main reason all this was happening. Baylor, who could now look at things from the outside, noticed what Wilt was doing.

"Wilt always has been capable of doing almost anything he wanted to do in this game," said Elgin. "And without tak-

Guard Jerry West is considered one of the great players of all time. *(Los Angeles Lakers)*

ing anything away from the other guys, I would say he is doing more things to help the team than ever before and is doing more that is responsible for the team's success than anyone else."

Laker Coach Bill Sharman had also become a big Chamberlain fan.

"Wilt makes an effort to get the guys up for every game," said Sharman. "In the game he does whatever is necessary to win. I don't need his scoring as much as his defense and rebounding. He's jamming up the middle and making the quick outlet pass to get the break going. Aside from Wilt, we have a small pro team so he has to bear a heavy burden for us, and he's doing it."

So the streak continued . . . 10, 11, 12, 13, 14. The NBA record was 20 and had been set by the Milwaukee Bucks the year before. They had topped the Knicks' record of 18 which had been set the year before that. Now the Lakers were making a run at it.

More than anything else, it was Wilt's play that astounded

everyone. Playing against Milwaukee, Abdul-Jabbar scored 39 on him, but Wilt got 26 rebounds and accounted for 23 points of his own, leading the Bucks center to call him "a remarkable man," and Milwaukee Coach Larry Costello to say that Wilt "doesn't seem like the same player."

Against Detroit and big Bob Lanier, Wilt scored 31 points and grabbed 32 rebounds. Lanier, a 6-11 giant himself, looked at Wilt and said, "It's like he's in his second childhood."

Finally the Lakers tied the record of 20 by beating Phoenix. Then they had to face the Atlanta Hawks at home in L.A. Once again it was Wilt leading the way. He blocked a shot of Jim Washington's so hard that Washington fell to the floor. Then big Walt Bellamy went up for a slam dunk and somehow Wilt got that one, too, his great strength almost tearing the ball out of the basket.

The Lakers were up by twelve with five minutes left. But suddenly things began turning around. The Hawks were coming and L.A. seemed to tense up, perhaps from the pressure. With just a minute left the lead was down to one. The Lakers had the ball and for one of the few times all year, Wilt actually called for it down low. Goodrich lobbed a pass in to the big man and Wilt just went high in the air and jammed it home, as the sell-out crowd exploded. From there the Lakers held on to win their twenty-first straight, a new NBA record.

"We all got a little tired," Wilt said afterward. "The pressure got to us and we stopped playing our game. We almost blew it. The whole thing has been tough and I'm glad it's over. I'm proud of our accomplishment."

With the record under wraps, it would stand to reason that the team might let down somewhat. But they didn't. They continued to win, and now the record seemed to be getting into the realm of the amazing. They were like a steamroller that couldn't be stopped, and neither could Wilt.

The team won its 25th straight against Philadelphia as Wilt amazed everyone with 32 points, 34 rebounds, and 12 blocked shots. Philly's Billy Cunningham, a former team-mate of Wilt's couldn't believe the performance.

"I would have had six more hoops if it wasn't for Wilt," Cunningham said. "Those were layups that I either shot differently or he blocked. And there were some rebounds I thought I had that he just lifted right off my fingertips."

On they went . . . to 33 games. That's when it finally ended. But 33 games! It was almost unbelievable. After all, the NBA played an 82-game schedule, so 33 games isn't far from half the season. The longest winning streak in baseball is just 26 games. The team was absolutely unreal. And it wasn't a patsy league. There were a number of strong teams and many outstanding players. Yet for 33 games, the Lakers rolled over all of them.

And the team didn't let down much after that. They continued to play brilliant basketball. When the season ended they had won their division by 18 games, compiling the best NBA record ever, 69-13. Ironically, the old record was 68-13, in 1966-67 and by the Philadelphia 76ers, led by . . . Wilt Chamberlain.

Goodrich had led the team in scoring with a 25.9 average. West was right behind at 25.8. Wilt led the league with 1,572 rebounds, a 19.2 average, and also topped everyone in field-goal percentage. Though he averaged just 14.8 points a game, he nevertheless hit at a .649 clip, showing he was taking only the good percentage shots when necessary. West also capped another brilliant season by leading the NBA in assists with 9.7 a game. But there was one thing left to prove. The playoffs were coming up, and that's where the team always seemed to flounder.

The conference semifinals were easy. The Lakers eliminated the Chicago Bulls in four straight games. Now they had to face the Milwaukee Bucks and Kareem Abdul-Jabbar. In the first game, the Bucks caught the Lakers flat and embarrassed them, 93-72. Were the Lakers going to come apart again?

Game two would be the barometer, and it was a brilliant game on both sides, the lead changing hands again and again. The Lakers shot very well, but Abdul-Jabbar was a one-man gang, connecting on his sky hook and other shots to the tune of forty points. Wilt had to work both ends just to keep up with the younger man.

The Lakers led by a point with seconds left. But Abdul-Jabbar surprised everyone by challenging West for the ball at midcourt. Jerry lost it and it was headed out of bounds when it hit one of the refs and stayed in. West grabbed it again and fired to Hairston, who put in the clinching hoop. L.A. won 135-134.

Game three was again close. L.A. held a point lead when the Bucks fouled Wilt. Always a poor foul shooter, Wilt was under real pressure. But he made both and the Lakers won by three, 108-105. Milwaukee managed to win game four, but the Lakers took the next two and made it to the finals.

Something else had emerged in their victory over the Bucks. Wilt had always been the villain, the Goliath who beat up on smaller men. But playing against the younger, more agile Abdul-Jabbar, Wilt suddenly became the sentimental favorite of the fans. After all the years, the big man appreciated it.

"I'm delighted to be looked at in a favorable way," he said. "A lot of people seem to be changing their minds about me, and I think it goes a little deeper that just rooting. I'm very grateful."

In the finals the Lakers would once again meet the New York Knicks. The New Yorkers only had the seventh-best record in the NBA, but had pulled together in the playoffs to whip Baltimore and Boston. They did it without their big center, Willis Reed, out with a knee injury. Jerry Lucas at 6-8 was the center, but the Knicks got by with beautiful teamwork, smart play, and good perimeter shooting. But with Wilt, the Lakers were heavy favorites.

Yet the first game of the finals surprised everyone. The

Knicks shot the eyes out of the basket. They couldn't miss. When it ended they had an easy 114-92 victory. But the Lakers reversed it in the second game, going inside more, and watching the Knicks' shooters come down to earth. They won, 106-92. Even more important was that the Knicks lost their top forward, Dave DeBusschere, with a rib-cage injury.

Game three was easy. L.A. built a 22-point lead and coasted home, 107-96. Game four was the best of the series, a nip-and-tuck battle that was tied at the end of regulation. But the Lakers were just too powerful and won it in overtime, 116-111. Wilt had hurt his right wrist in a fall early in the game. After it was over the pain became worse. He went for X rays.

There was no fracture, just a bad sprain. The doctors did not feel he could play in game five. But Wilt had been called a quitter before, and didn't want it to happen again. He treated the wrist with ice packs and heat, took an anti-inflammatory injection, and played with a padded wrap around the hand.

It didn't stop him. He played perhaps the game of his life, scoring 24 points and grabbing 29 rebounds. He seemed to be all over the court to harass the Knick shooters and block their shots. When it was over the Lakers had finally won a championship, 114-100, and Wilt was the Most Valuable Player.

It was the greatest moment in the history of the L.A. Lakers. The players and fans knew it wouldn't be a dynasty. Wilt was thirty-five, West thirty-three, and they were the keys to the team. But they had put it together for one season and dominated their sport. And along the way, they had that incredible 33-game win streak, one of the greatest records in the history of sport. It may never be broken.

And when it was all over, Jerry West summed up the remarkable season it had been for all of them.

"When we went to training camp last fall I thought we'd win our division, but never get past Chicago or Milwaukee into the finals. We were a team with a lot of lacks, but Coach Sharman fit us together perfectly. He told us he thought that if we played the way he wanted us to that we could beat any-one. He got us to believe that right away.

"And as for Wilt, he was simply the guy that got us there."

In the playoffs with the New York Knicks, Wilt battles burly Willis Reed (19), while Laker teammates Happy Hairston (right) and Jim McMillan (5) look on. *(Team Magazine)*

David Slays
Goliath

HIS NAME is David Thompson. No fancy or cute nicknames, nothing to describe the things he does on a basketball court. Just David Thompson. But very soon after he began playing varsity basketball for North Carolina State University in 1972, fans all across the country knew exactly who he was. He didn't need a nickname.

So that's David. But who is Goliath? In this case its the University of California at Los Angeles basketball team— UCLA. The Bruins, as they are called, had the most formidable college basketball dynasty in history. Beginning in the 1963-64 season, the Bruins, under coach John Wooden, astounded the basketball world by winning nine NCAA championships in ten seasons, the last seven coming in succession.

Plus they continued their winning ways with several different casts of characters. The first two Bruin titles featured a pair of slick guards, Walt Hazzard and Gail Goodrich. Then after a year's absence, they took up again, winning three

A relaxed David smiles for the camera. *(North Carolina State University)*

straight with big Lew Alcindor (now known as Kareem Abdul-Jabbar) in the middle and Mike Warren and Lucius Allen at guards. The other players were no slouches, either.

After Alcindor graduated, the team won two more with a pair of power forwards—Sidney Wicks and Curtis Rowe—leading the way. Then came two more under another supercenter, a guy named Bill Walton. And going into the 1973-74 season, the Bruins were highly favored to make it eight straight. Walton was back for his senior year and he hadn't played in a losing game since entering UCLA. It was hard to conceive of anyone's stopping them.

But rumblings were being heard from down Raleigh, North Carolina, way. That's where coach Norm Sloan was putting together a very solid Wolfpack team, led by a slender, 6-4 forward with the inconspicuous name of David Thompson.

What was so special about a slender, 6-4 forward? After

all, college basketball in the seventies was bigger and better than ever. There were plenty of fast, well-coordinated, muscular forwards standing 6-5, 6-6, 6-7, or even bigger, who should have no trouble putting a slender 6-4 forward in their hip pockets.

Now wait a minute. David Thompson was no ordinary player. Try this on for starters. David's vertical jump has been measured at 42 inches! That's right. David could get more than three feet off the floor with a single bound. And that put him in the stratosphere, high above players who were three, four, or five inches taller. Plus he was quick, with exquisite timing, a deadly jump shot, and superb instincts for the game. In other words, David Thompson was just about the most exciting player in the country. To many, he was tops. The only argument came from boosters of Bill Walton.

So it seemed almost inevitable that David Thompson and his Wolfpack teammates would have to meet up with the Walton Gang, the Goliaths of college basketball. And in the 1973-74 season, it happened.

First, let's take a look at how David and his teammates came together for their date with destiny. David was born in Shelby, North Carolina, on July 13, 1954, the last of eleven children. His parents, Vellie and Ida Thompson, were hardworking people who wanted nothing but the best for their children. They tried to instill in them values that would help them later in life.

When he was seven, David saw his fourteen-year-old brother, Vellie, Jr., shooting baskets on a new hoop in their backyard. That's all David needed. Basketball quickly became his first love, and he practiced for hours on end, day in and day out. He got better and better and was already quite a player when he reached the brand-new Crest High School. The basketball coach there was a man named Ed Peeler.

"Ed Peeler did a lot for getting black guys involved in athletics," said David. "If you had the ability to play, he made sure you played. And it didn't matter if you were black or white. Because of him there was no real trouble and a lot of guys with different backgrounds became friends."

And at the same time David Thompson was becoming a ballplayer. He often stayed well past midnight in the gymnasium, begging others to stay with him and play one more game, one more game. He already had his great leaping ability and was in the process of refining the rest of his skills. One night, early in his Crest High days, he was observed by a pro guard named Larry Brown, who would later coach David in the NBA. Brown saw David and quickly made a call to his old college coach, Dean Smith of North Carolina.

"Coach," said Brown, "I saw something tonight I just couldn't believe, a fourteen-and-a-half-year-old kid who's the most talented young player I've ever seen. He's got a flair about him that separates him from even the great players."

More and more people got the word about David as he starred for three seasons at Crest. When his senior year ended he went to play in the Marion North Carolina Civitan Classic, an all-star game featuring some of the best players in the state. David's team was a point down with just seconds remaining and one of his teammates was at the foul line with a chance to tie it.

David was lined up outside the lane. The shot caromed off the rim, bouncing away to the side opposite David. But he leaped in the air and across the width of the foul lane, stayed up and tapped the rebound in for the winning score. It was an almost impossible play, and those who saw it wondered if there was another player—high school, college, or pro—in the entire country who could have done it.

It was a spectacular end to David's high-school career. Now he had to pick a college, and there were plenty after him. It came as something of a surprise when he picked North Carolina State, traditionally not one of the nation's hoop powers.

"The year before I got there State signed a lot of other good young ballplayers," said David. "I felt my chances of winning a national championship would be better there. Plus I visited the campus and met some of the other players and really felt comfortable there."

So David arrived at N.C. State in the fall of 1971 and a new era in college basketball was about to begin. He tore things up as a freshman, was so spectacular with his tremendous leaps and all-around play that many fans began coming to the home games early just to see David and the freshman team play. He had a 35.6 average as a frosh, with a high game of 54, and at 6-4 still grabbed 13.6 rebounds a game. The varsity was 16-10 that year, and with the addition of David and a couple of his freshman teammates, looked forward to a big year in 1972-73.

Coming to the varsity with David were 5-7 floor-leader Monte Towe, guard Mo Rivers, and rebounding-forward Tim Stoddard. The center was a 7-4 junior giant, Tom Burleson, who, while lacking the consummate skills of a Bill Walton, was nevertheless a very good player who gave his all every game. There was one thing wrong even before the regular season began. The Wolfpack was on NCAA probation for some alleged recruiting violations. So they couldn't play in any postseason tournaments. They'd have to show their stuff in the regular season.

So the team played with a special kind of intensity right from the start. They won their early games against some smaller schools by big scores. It gave the young players a chance to know each other. Towe and David were beginning to perfect their "alley-oop" play where David would break to the hoop and leap high in the air, and Towe would loft a high pass toward the basket which David would catch in midair and slam dunk home. It was a spectacular maneuver, and the crowds, home or away, loved it.

When the Wolfpack began playing Atlantic Coast Conference rivals they were just as tough. After ten games they were unbeaten, and David was the most talked about sophomore in the country. The team was also ranked number three, behind

When the 6-4 Thompson leaps, he's usually well above the rim. Here he's on his way down after capturing a rebound. *(North Carolina State University)*

Walton and UCLA and behind ACC rival Maryland. Now in game eleven, they'd be meeting Maryland head-on.

David was averaging just under thirty points a game when N.C. State invaded College Park to meet Maryland. But there were some people saying he wasn't that good, that he had racked it up against the weaker schools. This game would tell.

It was a tough, emotional game from the beginning. David

was playing very well against the tall Terrapins, and at the half had his team in front by a 53-44 score. But Maryland fought back, led by its big men, Tom McMillen and Len Elmore. Finally they tied it, and then with four minutes left took an 85-83 lead. The crowd at Cole Field House was going wild.

Maryland then tried to stall. It might have been a mistake, because precious minutes ticked off. Then State got the ball back and promptly tied the game at 85 all. With 1:45 left, McMillen tried a shot that missed and Burleson took the rebound. Now the Wolfpack was back in the driver's seat.

Coach Sloan ordered his team to hold the ball. They did until the clock ran past the fifteen-second mark. With no set play and time running out, big Burleson found himself with the ball some twenty-five feet from the hoop. He had to shoot, and the ball bounced off the rim. Let David tell what happened next.

"I had faked and broken to the inside and was open," David said. "But Burleson didn't see me and took the shot. I had position on the boards and just went up. The ball was there."

David had gone high to grab the offensive rebound and put it back in for the winning basket. That made the final 87-85. The Wolfback was still unbeaten. And in what was a showcase game, David had scored thirty-seven big points. The win also elevated State to the number-two spot in the weekly polls, behind UCLA as usual. Both teams were unbeaten, though it was generally assumed that the Uclans with Bill Walton were the superior club. And because State was on probation there was no way the two clubs would meet during the 1972-73 season.

For the rest of the season N.C. State rolled. They beat Maryland again 89-78, and finished the regular campaign with a 25-0 record. And even though they couldn't go to the NCAA tourney, they nevertheless won the Atlantic Coast Conference playoff tournament for the nationals by beating Virginia, then Maryland once more 76-74. The greatest season in North Carolina State cage history had ended with the team 27-0.

As for David, he was undoubtedly the best sophmore in the country. In 27 games he had 666 points and a 24.7 average. He also had a 56.9 shooting percentage, showing he wasn't an indiscriminate gunner, and he grabbed 8.1 rebounds a game. He was also a unanimous all-America selection on all the major teams. The one thing that was missing was a crack at the national championship, which was won for the seventh straight year by also-unbeaten UCLA.

So David and his teammates looked to 1973-74. Not only would they be eligible for postseason play, but they were also scheduled to meet UCLA in the regular season. But the game was very early, in fact, the third game on the schedule. So after easy wins over East Carolina and Vermont, the Wolfpack traveled to St. Louis to meet the powerful Bruins on a neutral court.

The game was billed as a meeting between the two college basketball superpowers, but it turned out to be anything but that. UCLA was on its game and the Wolfpack wasn't. They just couldn't seem to sustain anything, while Walton dominated the boards and got the Bruins fast break rolling. UCLA took the lead early and built it slowly and steadily the rest of the way. The final was 84-66, a sound beating for a team that was supposed to be laying claim to the number-one ranking. The UCLA victory also broke the Wolfpack's winning streak at 29. It was a bitter defeat.

In addition, the Bruins held the three N.C. State stars in check. David had just 17 points and was not his usual spectacular self. Towe had 14 and was hounded by the quick UCLA guards, while Burleson only had 11 and was completely outplayed by the great Walton. One UCLA player called it "a real whippin' we gave them." And coach John Wooden also wanted the Wolfpack to remember it well.

"I want State to dwell on that eighteen-point margin," he said, as if anticipating another confrontation later in the year.

But the State players were also trying to keep the loss from becoming too big in their minds. As forward Tim Stoddard put it:

"We know they aren't eighteen points better than us. But what's more important is that *they* know it."

So the team pulled itself together and began winning once more. They were again an overpowering ball club with David leading the way. In their first meeting with Maryland that year David scored 41 points in an 80-74 victory, slam-dunking the ball on several occasions and bring the crowd to its feet. They rolled over everyone else after that, including Maryland once more, and finished the season with a 24-1 record, once again behind unbeaten UCLA in the polls.

But before the NCAA tourney, State had to get through its own ACC tournament. They took Virginia easily in the first game, 87-66, with David scoring 37 points. Now it was Maryland again. The Wolfpack had beaten the Terps five straight times over two seasons, but each game had been a war, several of them going down to the final seconds.

As usual, the two teams were locked in a struggle. The lead kept changing hands throughout the first and second halves. At the end of regulation time it was all tied. So the teams played a five-minute overtime and State's superior shooting finally paid off. They won it, 103-100, to retain their Atlantic Coast Conference title. Burleson had his greatest game against Maryland with 38 points, while David was his usual self with 29.

Then in the Eastern NCAA Regionals State whipped Providence 92-78 behind David's 40 points. Next came the Regional Final against Pittsburgh. State took an early lead and seemed to be on the way to an easy victory. Then midway through the first half, David went into his act again. He bolted across the lane and went way up in the air for an alley-oop. Only this time one of the Pitt players inadvertently hit him low and he did a cartwheel in the air and came down headfirst. He lay there motionless.

The crowd was absolutely silent as the players and coaches

gathered around David. He came to and was slowly helped to his feet and then from the court. The game had to go on. Playing without their star but with great intensity, the Wolfpack completed the victory, 100-72. David had scored just 8 points, but Burleson with 26, Towe with 19, and Mo Rivers with 17 picked up the slack.

And with about five minutes left in the game, David had reappeared, his head wrapped in a bandage which covered the fifteen stitches needed to close a large wound. He had a mild concussion, but no fracture. He would be able to play in the semifinals the next week. And he'd be needed there, because it was the big one. The Wolfpack would be meeting UCLA once again.

The game would be played in Greensboro, North Carolina, so State would have the crowd behind them. They were also anxious to prove their early-season 18-point loss to the Bruins was a fluke.

Both teams started slowly and carefully, not wanting to make any mistakes and give the other guy the early edge. There were just small leads, which opened, closed, and changed hands. No one was dominating. One good sign was that Burleson was playing Walton almost even, which had to be. And another positive note was that David showed no ill effects from his collision with the floor. He was once again leaping high without fear. So at halftime the score was tied at 35 all.

In the second half UCLA began to move out. When they opened an 11-point lead at 49-38, many of the fans thought it was the beginning of the end. There were visions of the first game early in the year which the Bruins had won so handily. But this time the Wolfpack wouldn't quit. Burleson made one beautiful play, stealing the ball from Walton after a rebound and putting it in. But the Bruins still wouldn't fold. They kept on an even keel and with eleven minutes remaining still held their 11-point lead at 57-46.

But then it was Monte Towe's turn. The little 5-7 guard began speeding the ball upcourt and feeding Burleson and David underneath. By fast-breaking, they were suddenly beating the Bruins at their own game. With Towe the catalyst, State reeled off 10 straight points to get themselves back in the game. Minutes later they pulled within one, 61-60.

They got the ball again and David cut toward the hoop. He showed that his fall hadn't affected him as he went a mile high, took a Towe pass, and slammed it home. He was fouled on the play and the free throw made it 63-61. State had the lead for the first time since the opening half.

Now the game settled into an epic battle, the upstart Wolfpack trying to knock off the longtime champs. With fifty-one seconds remaining, the score was tied at 65. UCLA got the ball in to Walton and he tried a hook shot. No good! Burleson rebounded and State held the ball, looking for a final shot. But as the clock wound down, the Bruin defense was magnificent and Stoddard had to force a shot from the corner. It missed, the buzzer sounded; the game would be going into overtime.

Both teams were being very cautious in the extra five-min-

UCLA's Bill Walton and David were college basketball's biggest superstars when their teams collided in the NCAA semifinals. *(UCLA)*

ute session. Each team scored once, but no more. Then with less than a minute remaining, Stoddard stole the ball from Greg Lee. State held it again. With ten seconds left, David drove toward the hoop. But at the last instant he passed the ball off to Burleson, who missed the shot. Again the buzzer sounded and again the two teams were tied, this time at 67. There would be a second overtime.

Now the strategy was different. Instead of playing it cautiously and holding the ball, both clubs decided to run and shoot. And it was the Uclans who were doing it better. With 3:27 left they had run up a 74-67 lead. How could State come back again?

But State tightened up defensively and began to hit shots of their own. The lead went to five, then three, then one. With about a minute left, David popped a jumper over Keith Wilkes, giving State the lead at 76-75, and the crowd went wild. UCLA couldn't score and the Pack had the ball again. This time Wilkes fouled David and his two free throws made it 78-75.

Now it was the Bruins who were coming apart, losing their poise. Once again they journeyed up the court but couldn't score. Now there were just twenty-seven seconds left. This time Burleson stole the ball. He got it to Towe, and Monte was fouled. His two free throws made it 80-75. The impossible was about to happen.

All the Bruins could manage was a last-second basket by Walton. The pack won it 80-77. UCLA's reign was ended. David had led the way with 28 points and 10 rebounds. Burleson had 20 and 14 rebounds, while Walton had another great game with 29 points and 18 rebounds. But it was the final result that counted.

The next night was almost anticlimactic. Playing Marquette in the championship game, the Pack seemed a little down at first, but rallied in the second half to win 76-64. Now it was official. They were national champions. It had taken them two years to prove their point, but they did.

David Thompson was all-everything again. He averaged

N.C. State's 1973-74 National Champions. David (44) is kneeling in the front row, fourth from right; Monty Towe (25) is kneeling, fifth from right; while Tom Burleson (24) is standing in the back row, second from left. *(North Carolina State University)*

26 points a game for the season, but rarely scored more than he had to for the victory. He was an all-American and was named college basketball's Player of the Year. Many people thought he'd pass up his senior year and turn pro right there. With Burleson graduating, the team would have little chance to repeat.

But David is not that kind of guy. He came back to average 29.9 points as a senior and lead the Pack to a 22-6 record and number-seven ranking in the country. He was Player of the Year once more. Then he went on to become just as great a pro with the Denver Nuggets.

Yet no matter where David's career takes him, many fans will remember the night in Greensboro, when David led his underdog teammates against the Goliath of college basketball, UCLA. And by coming out on top, the Pack showed the rest of the Davids of the world that no odds are too great if you want something badly enough.

Bill Walton
and Blazermania

THE 1970s has been a great decade for professional basketball. The National Basketball Association has grown and prospered. The existence of a second league, the American Basketball Association made it a player's market, and the pro hoopster was able to command huge, multiyear contracts. When the ABA folded and several of its teams came into the older NBA, pro ball was again on solid ground, bigger and better than ever.

As with most other sports, the pro basketball player in general has continued to improve. He is a man of immense natural talents, of inherent physical qualities that enable him to run and jump and shoot and do things that many of his predecessors could not do. But at the same time, the structure of the game, with the huge salaries and no-cut contracts, and free-agent situations, has made many of these men complacent. As good as today's players are, not all of them can be labeled winners.

Bill Walton as he appeared
during the Trail Blazers'
championship season.
(Portland Trail Blazers)

The winners are those who can adapt to the team concept, and that was the original premise put forth when the game was invented. There were plenty of superstars in the NBA during the 1970s, but for the most part the winning teams were those that had found the right combination, the delicate balance of offense and defense, and players willing to sacrifice individual statistics for a winning effort.

The dominant teams of the 1970s were largely the older, established clubs. The Boston Celtics, no longer the Bill Russell–led dynasty of the sixties, were nevertheless still a formidable ballclub with Dave Cowens at center. They took a pair of NBA titles in the seventies.

Then there were the New York Knicks. More than any other team of the seventies, perhaps the Knicks epitomized team play, unselfishness, and strong defense. Working around injuries to their star center, Willis Reed, the Knicks also won a pair of championships. The Golden State Warriors (formerly the Philadelphia Warriors) also won a title in a year when everything fell into place for the team.

Only one club in the early 1970s did not fit the mold. They were the Milwaukee Bucks, created as an expansion team in 1968-69, and an NBA champion in 1970-71. But the Bucks did it with a young supercenter, Lew Alcindor (now known as Kareem Abdul-Jabbar), and a veteran superstar guard, Oscar Robertson. The team did not have that fine balance the other title teams possessed, and as a result never repeated their achievement of that one year. Perhaps the other top clubs were all down at the same time.

At any rate, to many people nothing really new was happening in the NBA at the beginning of the 1976-77 season. The teams to watch were about the same, the Celtics, Warriors, perhaps the Knicks, the Washington Bullets, or the Los Angeles Lakers. The Lakers had also been a title team in the seventies, led by Jerry West and big Wilt Chamberlain. With Wilt retired, L.A. had traded for Kareem Abdul-Jabbar and was expected to dominate the Pacific Division of the NBA.

There was one team in the Pacific Division that wasn't expected to do much of anything. That was the Portland Trail Blazers. The Blazers were born to expansion in 1970-71. They picked up the co-Rookie of the Year in guard Geoff Petrie that season, but still finished last with a 29-53 record. The next season they again had the Rookie of the Year in 6-9 UCLA forward Sidney Wicks. Wicks had a big year, but Petrie was hurt and the team got even worse at 18-64.

In 1972-73 the two players were finally on the court at the same time, only to find they couldn't play together, couldn't blend their talents. Too often it was a case of hey-let-me-shoot, and the team remained in the cellar with a 21-61 record, although Wicks and Petrie both averaged twenty points a game. The next year the club was 27-55. So after four years, the Blazers weren't even able to match the losing record of their first year. Then something happened that made Portland fans believe the tide was about to change.

The Blazers drafted Bill Walton out of UCLA. The 6-11 redhead had been college basketball's premier big man for three seasons, leading the Uclans to a pair of NCAA titles with his hustling, aggressive, yet unselfish play. To many, he was the consummate center, a big man of all-around skills around whom a championship team could be built. He was seen as a player who didn't score as well as Abdul-Jabbar, didn't play defense as well as Bill Russell, didn't rebound as well as Wilt Chamberlain. Sounds negative, doesn't it? But he was so close to these other supercenters in all these categories, plus in passing he was said to be better than all of them, that he was viewed as potentially the finest big man ever to come into the National Basketball Association.

Many Trail Blazer fans figured the addition of Walton to the Wicks-Petrie duo would make the team an instant winner. Perhaps they could even challenge for the championship. When Walton signed a long-term $2.5 million contract with the team, the future of the Blazers seemed set.

But their first glance at the big guy from California left many Portland fans dumbstruck with surprise. Always a free spirit, Walton was now doing his own thing since he was out from under the tight reins of his college coach, John Wooden. He had let his flaming red hair grow long and tied it behind his head in a ponytail. In addition, he was sporting a new red beard, which was growing down the side of his face and under his chin.

Though never a huge man physically, Walton was nevertheless a wiry 230 pounds at UCLA. However he had recently switched over to a vegetarian diet, and whether that was the reason or not, reported to the Blazers some fifteen to twenty pounds underweight. He looked scrawny, almost emaciated, and there were people wondering if he could take the banging handed out in NBA games.

Yet Walton's first exhibition effort was a huge success. Playing against the Lakers, Bill totally dominated the game. The Blazers won it by a point, 92-91, as their rookie center scored 26 points and scrubbed the boards for 28 rebounds. It looked as if there was nothing to worry about.

Then Portland met the Bucks, who still had Kareem Abdul-Jabbar at the time. This time it was different. Abdul-Jabbar scored almost at will, while the younger man tried in vain to stop him. In the 27 minutes that they were on the court together, Kareem had 28 points and Walton had just 8. Bill did outrebound his opponent, 16-11, but the ease with which Kareem scored visibly upset him.

All Bill would say was, "He's the best I've ever seen. I really learned something out there tonight."

But some said Walton lost something out there. Soon after, he began playing badly. Other NBA centers, some with obvious lesser talent, were pushing him around. Finally, one of his friends said this:

"Bill was really depressed after the game against Kareem. He felt as if he was really whipped and this was something he wasn't used to. It never happened during his high school and college days. After that, players started pushing him around like a sheet of paper and he hardly fought back. It seemed as if his desire was fading fast."

So things began going from bad to worse for Bill and the Trail Blazers. For one thing, veteran players began teasing the youngster about his diet, his hair, his style of mountain-man clothing, his beard. And to make it worse, he wasn't producing on the court. Once the regular season started, it was the same old Blazers. Petrie and Wicks were taking turns gunning the ball and Walton was floundering underneath.

Everyone knew Walton was a team player and not used to the selfish antics of some pros. Sure enough, one night early in the season it hit the fan. Petrie took a long jump shot, which missed. Bill grabbed the rebound, called a timeout, and announced he couldn't play that kind of selfish basketball anymore.

Of course, he calmed down and kept playing. But pretty soon he began missing games, with illness and injury. Some of the other players felt he didn't really care, that he was sitting out whenever he felt like it. Finally a suspected bone spur on his foot really put him out of action. Bill's answer to almost all questions was simply, "It hurts," and his mates again thought he was dogging it. They also sniped at him when he refused to sit on the bench in street clothes during the games he missed. They said he didn't care about what happened to the team.

"It's not that," Bill explained. "It's just that I love basketball and get very emotionally involved both in practice and games. But when I'm not playing I don't get involved and not sitting on the bench is probably my way of controlling the frustrations of not playing."

The bone spur turned out to be something worse, strained ankle ligaments, which required a cast. So Bill was injured. As it turned out Bill played in just 35 of the team's 82 games, and the Blazers were losers again at 38-44. Everyone was disappointed and some expressed it, such as guard Geoff Petrie.

"The season was a disaster," said Petrie. "Bill was a real disappointment in his attitude and how he behaved. He didn't like the team or the city. He was aloof. We were thinking about winning a championship with him and the whole thing blew up in our faces."

Bill had a 12.8 scoring average and 12.6 rebounding average as a rookie. There was still hope for the next year, but in many ways it turned out to resemble the first. Bill didn't miss as many games, but there were enough minor injuries to keep him from getting into top condition and fully integrating with his teammates.

He missed 31 games in 1975-76, mainly due to a broken wrist. But in the 51 games he played, his scoring average was up to 16.1 and his rebounding to 13.3. There was still no doubt that the innate ability was there. The question was, would Bill ever stay healthy enough to harness it? And the team's 37-45 record that year didn't win any new converts to the Blazer fold.

It was obvious that changes had to be made. Some fans

and writers clamored for the team to trade Walton. Another year like the first two and he would no longer have even trading value. But the team's new coach, Jack Ramsay, had other ideas. He preferred to build around Walton and get rid of some of the other troublemakers.

Before the 1976-77 season, the club announced two major trades that would have tremendous significance. The first was with the Atlanta Hawks and sent Geoff Petrie packing in return for Atlanta's number-two draft choice in the ABA dispersal draft. These were players coming into the NBA from the folded ABA. The Blazers used the pick to grab Maurice Lucas, a 6-9 power forward who would be the perfect complement to Walton at center.

The second trade said good-bye to the controversial Sidney Wicks. So the club had rid itself of the two players who had led the franchise since the beginning. But with those two gone, Ramsay could now mold a unit that would play his way, as a team.

Second-year-pro Lionel Hollins took over as the leader in the backcourt. He was joined by ABA-refugee Dave Twardzik, veteran Herm Gilliam, and rookie speedster Johnny Davis. Joining Walton and Lucas on the front line was another second-year player, Bobby Gross, a 6-6 "small" forward who played with speed and intelligence. Lloyd Neal was an adequate forward-center, and Larry Steele could swing from backcourt to front. Two rookies rounded out the new-look Blazers. Now if only the big man could put it together.

One immediate difference was Bill's condition. He finally had an injury-free off-season and came to camp in shape. He also had his weight back up to 240 pounds. For the first time since very early in his rookie year, he seemed ready to play. He also hit it off with his new teammates and liked the renewed spirit on the Blazers.

"These are the kind of guys I'm used to playing with," he said. "This is going to be fun!"

That was a good sign. And the way the Blazers came out of the gate, they looked like a whole new team. And in a sense, they were. The team won four of its first five games and suddenly Bill Walton was the same kind of dominating center he'd been in college. He was playing with that old-fashioned intensity that characterized his years at UCLA.

A tiger on both backboards, Bill was triggering the fast break and hustling downcourt with the rest of the team. His passing was spectacular, and it seemed as if he scored just what was needed to have the team win. If everyone else was hitting, he was content to pass. If the others were off, he'd shoot more. Walton was still the epitome of the unselfish player.

Despite the fast start, Blazer fans were skeptical. They had

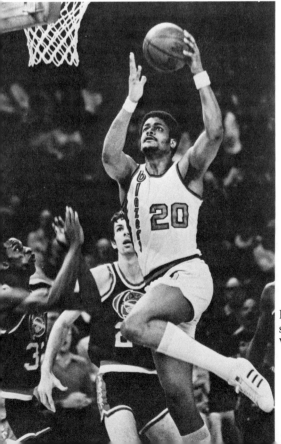

Power forward Maurice Lucas shared the rebounding load with Walton. *(Portland Trail Blazers)*

had too many disappointments during the short history of the franchise. So when the powerful Philadelphia 76ers came into Portland on November 5, everyone pointed to that game as the barometer. It would show if the Blazers were for real. The Sixers were a talented bunch, led by forwards Julius Erving and George McGinnis, and guard Doug Collins. They played run and gun, and did it well.

But the Blazers came out blazing. Lionel Hollins started it off with a jumper. Then Maurice Lucas took over, scoring seven straight points and giving Portland an early lead. Minutes later the Sixers started coming to life. They got a rebound and took off on a fast break, giving the ball to Erving, the fabulous Dr. J.

Taking huge strides, the Doctor drove past Bobby Gross and headed for the hoop and a showdown with Bill Watson. As Julius went up, Bill went up with him. The Doctor unveiled his magic, switching hands, pumping once, and hanging in the air as only he can do. But when he was ready to slam the ball home, he suddenly found Walton up there waiting for him. Bill smashed the ball back to the court and the huge Portland crowd went wild.

With the big center leading the way, Portland then proceeded to blow the Sixers off the court. The final score was 146-104. It was hard to believe. Suddenly the Blazers looked like a team, a powerhouse. As for Walton, he had played just 32 minutes, hit on 10 of 13 from the floor and 6 of 7 from the line for 26 points. He had 16 rebounds and handed off for 6 assists. While he was in the game, he dominated. As Philly forward George McGinnis said:

"Bill did everything out there. But he did it within a team concept. That's what impressed me the most. He's a total team player."

That was no surprise to Bill's old friends and former college teammates. He had always been a team player, and now that he had a solid supporting cast, they reasoned that the Blazers should remain a formidable lot. And they were right. The team didn't blow all their opponents out by forty-two points, but they were winning and winning big. They took over the divisional lead and caught the imagination of their hometown fans and indeed fans from all over the country.

In Portland, Blazermania became the byword, as the whole city began rooting for its Cinderella team with the big, redheaded center. After all, here was a team that hadn't produced a winner in its short history. Now there was talk of its challenging for an NBA title. And the fans had also waited three years for the real Bill Walton to stand up. Now, it appeared, he had.

By midseason the Blazers were still leading the division and Bill was atop the league in rebounding and blocked shots. Maurice Lucas was playing an all-pro-caliber forward and players like Hollins, Gross, and some of the others, unknown quantities before the season, were proving to be formidable NBA stars.

Walton was then chosen starting center for the West in the All-Star game and people were already comparing him with the likes of Russell, Chamberlain, and Abdul-Jabbar. The difference in his play from his first two years was amazing. Perhaps it was Philly's George McGinnis who expressed it best.

"This year Bill is healthy," said big George. "You can't play good if you don't feel good. But it's more than that. Last year he wouldn't get the ball. Now when he asks for it he gets it. There's no doubt in anybody's mind who the man is. When you're the man, you put out special. I heard one guy on television say he saw Walton's talent all the time. Who in the hell didn't see it?"

At the outset of the second half of the season the Blazers continued to roll. It seemed as if nothing could stop the Blazermania Express. But the one thing that could happen, did happen. Bill sprained his left ankle. He was anxious to get back in, but also wanted to be sure the ankle was healed for the stretch run. He missed seventeen games.

During that time, the Blazers were not the same team.

There was no way to replace the big man. The team won just 5 of the games without Bill and lost 12 of them. And during that period, the Lakers, led by Kareem Abdul-Jabbar, took over first place in the division. Even when Bill got back, the Lakers held on, though the Blazers were once again winning big. The team finished with a 49-33 record, best by far in its history. But they were in second place, four games behind L.A. Had Bill not been injured, the team would most likely have finished on top.

Still, Walton appeared in 65 games, scoring 1,210 points for an 18.6 average. He was second on the club to Lucas's 20.2. He also had the best rebounding average in the league, grabbing 14.4 a game, and was tops in blocked shots with 3.2 per game. Plus he was the starting center on the NBA's All-Defensive Team and finished just behind Abdul-Jabbar on the league's All-Star Team and in voting for Most Valuable Player. Many fans felt he should have taken the latter prize. But all Bill worried about was the playoffs. He wanted to prove his team was for real.

The first round was a two-of-three against the Chicago Bulls. The Blazers won the first and third games to take the series and move into a best-of-seven meeting with the tough Denver Nuggets. The Nuggets had come into the NBA from the ABA, the franchise intact, and promptly won its division with a 50-32 record. It wouldn't be an easy series for the Blazers. The Nuggets had a superstar in David Thompson and some fine talent.

Game one was played in Denver, and the Blazers quickly wiped out the home-court advantage with a 101-100 victory. The Nuggets won game two, but the Blazers took the next two on their home court for a 3-1 lead. They lost the fifth, but then wrapped it up with an easy victory in the sixth game. Now it was the division finals against the Lakers and this one would put Bill Walton up against Kareem Abdul-Jabbar. Bill didn't want to make any comparisons between himself and his rival.

"All I'll say about Kareem is that he's playing the best basketball of his life and I have to play well for us to do well against them."

Portland coach Jack Ramsay, however, favored Walton and the Blazer style of play.

"I like my own player," said the coach. "Kareem is superb. He makes their other players better. But Bill's performance is straight across the board. He doesn't have to get forty for us to win. He can get fifteen as long as he distributes the ball."

Game one was easy. The Lakers were a tired team after a hard-fought series against Golden State which ended the night before. Portland just rolled, 121-109. Walton was one of four Portland players with more than 20 points and he added 13 rebounds. He also picked up 6 assists to lead the Portland fast break.

Game two was also played at Los Angeles and it was a lot tougher. Abdul-Jabbar was hitting his famous "sky hook," and no one on earth can stop that. But the team play of the Blazers offset the big man's scoring and Portland managed to win it at the end 99-97, to go two up. Kareem had 40 points, but Bill took care of the boards with 17 rebounds.

The third game at Portland was another close one. Blazer-mania had really gripped the city by now and the arena was packed, with those who couldn't get in following the game on radio. At the end of the third quarter the Lakers had a 75-73 lead. But in the final session Bill took over. He hit for 14 of his 22 points in the last twelve minutes to enable Portland to emerge with a 102-97 victory. They were now three games up and looking for a sweep.

Game four was another great team effort by the Blazers. Lucas, Davis, Hollis, and Walton all played very well. The Lakers fought hard but just couldn't seem to put it together in the final minutes, when it counted. Portland prevailed once more, 105-101. Now the Blazers were in the final, and all that stood between them and a storybook season were the Philadelphia 76ers.

Everyone knew about the Sixers. That made the final meeting even more interesting. It would be one-on-one versus team basketball. As powerful as the Sixers were, with their great individual stars, team basketball had a way of prevailing in the NBA. Still, many people found it difficult to pick against Erving, McGinnis, and company.

Game one was in Philadelphia, the third straight series the Blazers had started on their opponent's home court. The last two times they had immediately offset the advantage by winning, but this time they didn't. Philly got off the mark fast and ran its way to a 107-101 victory. Erving and Doug Collins had super games with 33 and 30 points respectively. They needed those efforts, because Bill was superb for Portland with 28 points and 20 rebounds. Had it not been for 34 Blazer turnovers, the end result might have been different.

Yet game two turned into another disaster. Maurice Lucas got into a brawl with Philly's kid center, Darryl Dawkins, and both were thrown out of the game. Philly kept running its fast break and won pulling away, 107-89. The Blazers looked inept and disorganized. A confident Julius Erving said that his club was showing that a well-drilled team couldn't necessarily pick the Sixers apart. But Portland veteran Herm Gilliam insisted his team wasn't yet playing its game.

So it was back to Portland and a must game. If Philly won again it would be all but over. But right from the beginning of the game it looked like a different Blazer team. They were moving and cutting, and Bill Walton was throwing some unbelievable passes, hitting his teammates underneath time and time again for easy layups. Now it was the 76ers making the mistakes, missing the shots, and looking like a very bad schoolyard team instead of top pros.

The Blazers rolled to an early lead, only to have Philly slowly close the gap in the middle periods. But in the fourth the Blazers broke loose and ran away to a 127-109 victory. Bill had 20 points and 18 rebounds. Lucas scored 27, Gross

19, and Johnny Davis 18. It was a complete team effort and it set the pattern for the rest of the series.

In the fourth game the Blazers again took an early lead only to see Philly battle back. Only this time the third period was crucial. Bill began to hit his teammates with pretty passes once more as the Blazers began surging. Then he picked up his fifth foul and had to sit down. But even without their big center, the Blazers outplayed the Sixers. It seemed as if Philly was just coming apart. The onslaught continued right to the end. What had been a 48-46 game at the half ended in a 130-98 Portland rout. The series was tied at two games each and heading back to Philly.

Now the crucial game. The winner of this one would be in the driver's seat. The Sixers thought they could turn it back

Guard Lionel Hollins ran the team from the backcourt. *(Portland Trail Blazers)*

around at home, but soon a familiar pattern emerged. The game was close in the first half, but in the third period the Blazers took it to the Sixers once again. It was the same pattern, Walton getting rebounds and triggering the fast break, blocking up the middle to stop the Philly offense, and hitting his cutting teammates with precision passes.

Led by Erving, the Sixers made a brief comeback in the final session, but fell short, 110-104. Walton had 24 rebounds and his club had a three games to two lead. One more win and they would be NBA champions. And they'd have a chance to do it in front of the Blazermania-mad crowd in Portland.

But this game would be a battle. The Sixers weren't about to lie down and die. They still felt they were the better team. At the end of one quarter the game was tied at 27 all, and the Blazers knew they were in for a battle. With Walton controlling the boards, Portland then pulled to a 67-55 halftime lead. But the Sixers didn't fold. With Erving and McGinnis hitting on jump shots and drives, Philly pulled within 8 with just 2:20 left. Two more baskets by the Doctor and a foul shot by Lloyd Free cut it to 3.

Then Maurice Lucas hit a free throw to bring it to 4, but a hoop by McGinnis made it 109-107. There were just eighteen seconds remaining. The Blazers tried to hold it, but couldn't. Philly had the ball with seconds left. Erving tried a twenty-footer. It missed! McGinnis got the rebound. George went up from fifteen feet out. It was off the rim! Walton deflected the ball to Hollins. The clock ran out. The Portland Trail Blazers were world champions!

What a Cinderella story it had been. The Blazers had come from nowhere to take the NBA title. But they did it with a formula that had been successful for years. A balance of offense and defense, unselfish team play with contributions from everyone, and a supercenter who could take control of a game and put it in his hip pocket. Bill Walton had 20 points and 23 rebounds in the final game and was named Most Valuable Player in the playoffs.

Bill enjoyed the victory as much as anything else he had ever done in sports. For a professional athlete who was disgruntled much of his first two seasons, he surprised everyone by saying:

"This is the most fun I've ever had in any sport since I started playing when I was eight years old!"

Someone was quick to point out that the average age of the Trail Blazers was just twenty-three years. With a player like Walton and the talented youth around him, it was thought the Blazers would be winning for years. And, indeed, at the outset of the 1977-78 season they appeared to be by far the best team in basketball. But then the injuries started. Lucas was hurt, Bobby Gross was hurt, and a couple of others as well. Then Bill Walton sustained a foot injury which didn't respond.

By playoff time the team seemed pretty much intact. But then it was discovered that Bill had a broken bone in his foot. He had to sit, and the team was eliminated by the Seattle Super Sonics. Blazermania was over. And after the season it was learned that Walton was unhappy with some of the medical practices on the team. His injured foot might keep him out a whole year. He decided to leave Portland and sign with another club.

The Blazers should still have a fine team. Whether they can ever recapture the moment of 1976-77 remains to be seen. In today's sports world it's hard to keep a team intact and winning. But for one brief shining moment in the spring of 1977, the Portland Trail Blazers captured the fancy of the basketball world.

Bobby Orr,
the Greatest Ever

BOBBY ORR is not an event; he is a person. He is also a hockey player, and in the eyes of many, the greatest hockey player ever to lace on a pair of skates. What makes it even more amazing is that most people reached that conclusion by the time Bobby Orr was all of twenty-four years old.

Unfortunately, the Bobby Orr story is not only one of triumph, it is one of tragedy, though perhaps the final chapters have not yet been written. For while Bobby Orr was being called the greatest ever by the time he was twenty-four, he was just twenty-eight years old when it appeared his career was over.

It was his left knee that betrayed Bobby, a knee cut into six times by surgeons trying to repair it. Bobby's last productive season was 1974-75. The next year he played in just ten games before the knee went out again. He sat out almost all of 1976-77 and all of 1977-78. Then in 1978-79 he tried it once more, but after a handful of games he called it quits for good. The knee just couldn't take it. And even before that, it was obvious that Bobby would never be what he once was.

What Bobby Orr was is difficult to describe, because he was so many things on the ice. He was a dominating hockey player of many diverse skills. Not only that, he completely revolutionized the game, because he played his position in a way that had not really been done before.

Bobby was a defenseman. Until he came along, almost all the superplayers in hockey had been forwards. Ask about the all-time greats of the game and you would get names like Howie Morenz, Gordie Howe, Maurice "The Rocket" Richard, Jean Beliveau, Bobby Hull—all forwards, all big goal scorers. Defensemen were always considered separately.

Though forced out of hockey by injuries before his thirtieth birthday, Bobby Orr is considered by most people to be the greatest player ever. *(Boston Bruins)*

Players like Eddie Shore and Doug Harvey were certainly all-time greats, but their job was to stop the opposing forwards from scoring, and they did it well.

When Bobby came along, defensemen still played that way. They hung back, played defense, checked the forwards, blocked shots, and tried to get the puck. When they did get it they'd quickly pass it to one of their forwards, then hang back so as not to be caught out of position up ice.

Bobby played defense, too. But when he got the puck, he took it up ice, sometimes rushing the entire length of the rink, stickhandling beautifully through opposing forwards and defensemen. He became part of the offense, an integral part. In deep, he could make the play, or take the shot himself. He could do this because he was a player of multiple skills.

He handled the puck as well as anyone. Sometimes it seemed like it was attached to his stick. He had incredible skating ability, enabling him to stop and start, to pivot and turn, to maneuver in ways that other players could not. And he had speed, speed to get back on defense even when he was way up ice in the attacking zone.

In addition, he had a blistering but accurate shot, a shot that would have been totally wasted had he laid back and just played the traditional kind of defense. Bobby joined the Boston Bruins when he was just eighteen. That was in 1966-67. He reached his peak in the early 1970s and dominated the game until his knee would allow him to go on no longer.

He was born in Parry Sound, Ontario, Canada, on March 20, 1948. Like so many Canadian youngsters, he learned to play hockey very early, and it wasn't long before people began noticing his superior skills. The Bruins set their sights on him when he was still a young teenager, and signed him to a future contract right then. That's something that cannot be done today. But in those days a team could sign a player when he was still very young. He would then leave home and do very little but play hockey until he was ready for a shot at the NHL This system is no longer used, because the players who didn't make it were often left without much education and no other skills.

That wouldn't be the case with Bobby Orr. He joined the Bruins in 1966-67 and immediately became a regular. Though he was just eighteen, his skating ability and talents were obvious to everyone. He wasn't afraid to take charge and he wouldn't be intimidated by the veteran players, even if it meant fighting. In 61 games his rookie year he scored 13 goals and had 28 assists for 41 points. He was named the league's Rookie of the Year and was named to the second-team league All-Stars.

The next year he played in just 46 games due to the knee, scoring just 11 goals and 20 assists for 31 points. Yet so obvious was his talent that he won the James Norris Trophy as the best defenseman in the league and was a first-team All-Star selection. That was significant in that Bobby Orr went on to win the Norris Trophy eight straight years until the knee injury knocked him out of action. He was also a first-team selection those eight years.

Bobby wasn't the only star on the Bruins. The team was building to one of the best in the league. Center Phil Esposito was becoming a virtual scoring machine up front, with Bobby's help, of course, and players like John Bucyck and John Mckensie represented a rough-tough style of play that made the Bruins a feared team throughout the league.

In 1969-70 Bobby astounded the hockey world by scoring 33 goals and 87 assists for 120 points. All were records for a defenseman, and he was also the first defenseman ever to lead the league in scoring. Boston went on to win the Stanley Cup that year with Bobby scoring 9 goals and 11 assists in 14 Cup games.

When it was all over, he was named the league's Most Valuable Player and the Most Valuable Player in the playoffs. The next year he did even better, with 37 goals and a record of l02 assists for 139 points. And that same year Esposito set all kinds of records with 76 goals and 76 assists for 152 points. Orr and Esposito were the talk of the hockey world. But the Bruins didn't win the Cup that year and vowed to regain it in 1971-72.

By then, other hockey people, past and present, were in total awe of Bobby Orr. The superlatives were incredible for a twenty-four year-old athlete. Here is a sampling just to show what his peers thought of him. This is important, because those too young to have seen Bobby play in his prime won't really be able to imagine how good he was.

Bobby Hull, the NHL's top superstar before Orr, had this to say.

"Orr is the greatest young hockey player to come along since I've been here. He controls the puck. If he doesn't have the room to skate with it he'll give it to a teammate and then bust to get it back. Most guys, after they've given it up, will just watch it go. Bobby takes off and when he hits your blue line he's streaking."

Glen Sather, a former teammate of Bobby's, put it this way.

"He doesn't beat you because he's Bobby Orr. He beats you because he's the best. He's the best thing that ever happened to hockey. And he's the best conditioned athlete I've ever seen. There's absolutely no fat under his skin. It would be interesting to see where his strength comes from. He wears the same size clothes I do—43 jacket, 31 waist—but he weighs 20 pounds more than I do."

No one can watch what's happening on the ice better than the goalie. Jacques Plante, the top goalie of the last era, and Ken Dryden, one of the tops today, both have definite opinions about Bobby Orr.

Said Plante, "You say about each of the great players: He's a good skater, or a particularly good stickhandler, or he has a great shot, but something is always missing. Bobby Orr has it all. He is the best I've seen—ever. He does everything right. In front of his own net every other defenseman will have a blind side, or will miss something that's developing behind him. But Bobby Orr is unreal. He sees everything. Plus he's got a mean streak, which makes him a lot better."

This is what Ken Dryden had to say. "It's different from any other sport. You'd always get a real strong argument about who's best in baseball or in basketball. But Orr is so clearly the best in hockey. I don't know that there's ever been anybody that so completely dominated a team sport."

Despite the success and adulation that came at an early age, Bobby always kept a low profile and guarded his private life quite zealously.

"I never think of myself as an idol," he has said. "I'm a hockey player. I enjoy hockey. When I quit it will be because I don't enjoy it anymore."

As expected, the Bruins won their division in 1971-72, and then went out to regain the Stanley Cup. Orr was his usual self in the regular season, with 37 goals and 80 assists for 117 points. Esposito had 66 goals and 67 assists for a league-leading 133. They were again the most potent one-two punch in hockey.

The Bruins reached the finals without too much trouble. They were rolling. Now they had to play their arch rivals, the New York Rangers. New York was seeking its first Cup since 1939-40. They were hungry. But they usually had all kinds of trouble with the Bruins, who won five straight from them in the regular season by a combined score of 24-4.

To many, it was a confrontation of the boxer and the puncher. The Rangers were a finesse team with a reputation for not liking a physical game. The Bruins were often described as a bunch of muggers and they liked to work the Rangers over. But despite the lopsided scores from the season, Bobby Orr sounded a warning to his teammates.

"I hope we learned a good lesson last year when Montreal upset us in the playoffs," he said. "We're beginning a new season. Nothing that happened before really counts."

The first game was a wild one. Boston raced to a 5-1 lead as the hometown Bruin fans went wild. But the Rangers made it 5-2 before the second period ended. Then they scored three unanswered goals to tie the game at 5-5 at 9:17 of the third session. But with just 2:16 remaining, a second-line Boston player named "Ace" Bailey scored the winning goal. Boston had a one-game lead.

By this time, everyone knew that Bobby was playing on a very painful left knee, a knee that would need another operation when the season was over. But to watch him you'd never know it. He skated with his usual dexterity, ignoring the pain and playing his game.

Boston won the second game, but the Rangers came back

Center Phil Esposito teamed with Bobby to give the Bruins an unstoppable one-two scoring punch. *(Boston Bruins)*

to take the third game in New York. In game four the Rangers contained all the Bruins except one—Bobby Orr. Bobby had two goals and an assist as Boston won 3-2, to take a 3-1 lead. They were leading the fifth game, 2-1, when the Rangers suddenly came back to win, 3-2, making it also a 3-2 series. The sixth game was to be played at Madison Square Garden and the Rangers had new hope.

In the first period Boston got a man advantage on a Ranger penalty. The puck came back to Bobby at the blue line. A Ranger came at him, but Bobby pivoted on the sore left knee and sped away. He moved within thirty-five feet or so of Ranger goalie Gilles Villemure and let go a low, hard shot. It passed between Villemure's left leg and the post for the first score of the game.

Early in the second period Bobby showed his stuff again. The Bruins were shorthanded for three minutes and twenty-two seconds, forty-eight seconds of which they were two men down. Yet Bobby controlled the puck much of the time, playing keepaway from the frustrated Rangers, skating and whirling, sprinting and pivoting, making the puck dance on his stick like a yo-yo. The Rangers couldn't score.

It was still a 1-0 game after two periods. Early in the third period Bobby got the puck again. Wayne Cashman, a Boston winger, remembers what Bobby had said earlier.

"Bobby had told me he was shooting to Villemure's right too often. He said Villemure was handling these shots without much trouble. So he told me to stay to Gilles' left side and be ready for a tip-in."

Sure enough, Bobby fired a slap shot and Cashman was right there. The puck deflected off his stick and into the goal. It was 2-0. Later in the period Cashman scored again making it 3-0, and that's the way it ended. The Bruins were champions once more.

Bobby was very happy after the game. He said his teammates played perfectly. "We were on top of them for 60 minutes. They had no place to go." But he also admitted the knee was bothering him as the series unfolded.

"Sure, it got sore," he said. "It gave out sometimes when I made a sharp cut to change directions. It even locked on me at times, so I didn't rush the puck as often as I used to. Maybe I'm just getting lazy."

Anyone who saw Bobby play would find that hard to believe. The Rangers' Vic Hadfield complained, "The guy (Orr) always had it (the puck). And when he had it there wasn't a thing we could do about it."

But perhaps it was Bobby's teammate, Derek Sanderson, who summed it up best.

"The way I saw it," said Derek, "Bobby controlled the puck for 40 minutes and was nice enough to let the other 35 players in the game use it for the other 20. He's not a selfish kid, you know."

No, just an incredible hockey player. Bobby had 5 goals and 19 assists in 15 playoff games that year. And when the season ended he swept all the prizes again. He was an All-Star, won the Norris Trophy as best defenseman, the Hart Trophy as Most Valuable Player, and the Conn Smythe Trophy as MVP in the playoffs.

Despite the operation in the offseason he played in 63 games the next year and had 29 goals and 72 assists. The year after he had 32 goals and 90 assists. And in 1974-75, he seemed better than ever. Playing in 80 games he set another incredible record by scoring 46 goals as a defenseman, adding 89 assists, and leading the league in scoring with 135 points. He was just twenty-seven years old. But while he was better than ever, the knee was worse.

The next year he was in just ten games. Feeling that he was finished, the Bruins accepted an offer from the Chicago Black Hawks and sent Bobby over. Bobby got a new, multimillion-dollar contract, but said he wouldn't take the money if he couldn't play. He had his sixth operation and waited. There was no way he could play in '77-78. No one thought he'd ever play again. But Bobby was determined.

"I'm just thirty years old. Until now 1 couldn't accept the

fact that I'd never play again," he said. "Now I can accept it. But I've had a long layoff and I'm going to try once more. They say I can't do any further damage to the knee. I just don't feel I'd be fair to myself and the Black Hawks if I didn't try it one more time."

So that's what Bobby did in 1978-79. At first there was optimism. Bobby was very rusty. He hadn't played in two years and, in effect, had to relearn the game as a player. But the knee seemed all right. In fact, he was beginning to show some flashes of the old Orr and there were even a couple of goals. But that's all it was. Flashes. Before long the knee began troubling him again. It just couldn't take the pounding and wear of game conditions. Finally, the inevitable announcement came.

"I know now that I cannot play hockey any longer," Bobby said, wiping away the tears. "This time I am retiring for good."

A sports tragedy? Perhaps. But then there were the magnificent years with the Bruins, years in which Bobby Orr left a permanent mark on the sport of hockey. And while many young defensemen try to copy his style of play, none of them can do it quite like the master. Bobby Orr was special, the kind of player who comes along once in a lifetime.

Three Straight
for Bjorn

SOME PEOPLE call him the Ice Man because of his unchanging, unemotional demeanor on the tennis court. Others talk about his personality or lack of it, because he rarely says much and is not at all controversial. Still others wonder if he can really be as young as the calendar says he is. But none of the above will dispute one undeniable fact. Bjorn Borg is one great tennis player.

Playing in a sport that now has more top-flight competitors and is bigger and better than ever before, the blond-haired native of Sweden has gone to the head of the class. And if it weren't for a battling, stubborn, tenacious American named Jimmy Connors, Borg would be unanimously acclaimed as the world's best. The way things stand as of 1978, opinion is just about evenly split as to which player is the best.

To some, Borg's rise to the top is more amazing than Connors's in that it happened at an earlier age (by about three years) and because he comes from a country that is not known for producing many world-class athletes.

This is the kind of shotmaking that helped Bjorn win three straight Wimbledon titles, 1976-78. *(United States Tennis Association)*

But whether you are a Borg fan or a Connors supporter, one thing cannot be ignored. In 1978, Bjorn Borg won the Wimbledon Tennis Tournament singles title for the third consecutive year, a feat that had not been accomplished in some thirty-two years.

Wimbledon is still considered the most prestigious tourney of them all, the one with the most tradition and the most glamour, and the most difficult to win. Just look at the list of players who have won two straight, but failed to make it three. The list reads like a Who's Who of tennis history: Don Budge, Lew Hoad, Rod Laver, Roy Emerson, Laver a second time, and John Newcombe. Not a pattycake player in the bunch.

The only man to do it three times was England's Fred Perry from 1934 through 1936. Without taking anything away from Perry, there weren't nearly as many top-flight players back then trying to knock off the champ. What makes it even more incredible is that Borg won his first in 1976 at the age of twenty, and his third at the ripe old age of twenty-two. With that track record there's no telling how long he'll go on.

When the decade of the 1970s began, the holdovers from

the sixties still dominated the sport, players like Ken Rosewall, Laver, Arthur Ashe, and Newcombe. But by the middle
seventies, two young players had come along to take charge,
Borg and Connors. And they provided a startling contrast
which made their rivalry even more interesting.

Connors was the American, brash, cocky, outspoken, emotional, a hard-hitting fighter with an obvious killer instinct, a
guy who didn't like to lose and played every point as if the
match were on the line. He often complained about calls and
carried on in what some considered an unprofessional man-
ner. But you had to say one thing about Connors; he let it all
hang out.

Borg, on the other hand, was looked upon as the cold, unemotional Swede, a youngster who said little and whose demeanor on the court betrayed little of what was churning inside him. He rarely questioned a line call, even if it was
obviously wrong, rarely allowed himself to be affected by the
partialities of the fans. He played his tennis with great skill
and an inner intensity that produced the same killer instinct
which was so obvious in Connors.

Bjorn Borg was born on June 6, 1956, in a small town near
Stockholm, Sweden. Bjorn remembers being competitive
when only a small boy and playing games of darts with his
family.

"I cried when I lost," he says. "Then they would let me win
and I would get my confidence back."

There's a story that his father, Rune Borg, won a tennis
racket in a Ping-Pong tournament and gave it to his son, who
began practicing with it whenever he could. He already had
his two-hand backhand style because he wasn't big or strong
enough to hit with one hand. When he was ten he was spotted by a man named Percy Rosburg, who was looking for
young prospects.

"He hit his forehand the same way he does now," recalls
Rosburg, "all wrist, like a ping pong shot. But I had to run
well, even then, to get it back. He didn't know how to serve

and he kept bothering me with questions. But there was a look in his eyes. I remember we wanted to change the two-hand shot, but he could put the ball where he wanted it so we left it alone. And oh, how he hit so hard and fought like hell, even then."

It wasn't long before Bjorn was the top young prospect in the country. When he was thirteen he was playing in an age-group tourney and was entered in several classes. One day he was on the court for eleven hours, playing nine matches and reaching the finals of five different classes. He won in the fourteen-and-under group.

Shortly after that he began winning junior titles and tour-naments in different parts of the world. In 1972 at the junior Wimbledon, he fought back from a 5-2 deficit in the final set against Englishman Buster Mottram and won the title. And by the time he was fifteen he began playing in Davis Cup matches for his country.

By 1973 he was already beating some of the world's best players. He had a steady game with strong baseline strokes, his two-hand backhand and top-spin forehand which made the ball kick up when it hit. He also seemed to play well on all surfaces from the lightning-fast grass court to the much slower clay. He worked hard and continued to improve.

Bjorn had left school after the eighth grade to concentrate on tennis. He could do this because he already knew he had exceptional talent. For the average youngster that would be a mistake. He was a pro by seventeen and signed to play on the tough WCT tour. And when he was still seventeen he won matches against Ilie Nastase and Jimmy Connors, to name just two. A short time later he defeated Arthur Ashe, Roscoe Tanner, and Mark Cox to win his first pro tourney in Eng-land.

He continued playing, and amazingly enough, by mid-1974 his record against the seven acknowledged top players in the world—Newcombe, Nastase, Stan Smith, Ashe, Laver, Connors, and Rosewall—was nine wins and nine losses. He was coming fast.

Rod Laver, for one, was amazed at Borg's progress. He was all ready to offer the youngster some advice until he remembered himself at that age.

"I was going to advise him not to play so often," said the Rocket, "not because of his health, but because of his mind. The poor kid will go nutty, I thought, be drained of interest. But then I remembered when I was eighteen, all I wanted to do was play and hit the ball, too."

In 1974 Bjorn got to the finals of the WCT, a prestigious round-robin-type tournament, but lost to John Newcombe. He lost again the following year to Arthur Ashe. Newk had been rated number one in the world in '74 and Ashe in '75. But Bjorn was gaining on them. So was Connors, who didn't play WCT but had won both Wimbledon and the U.S. title at Forest Hills in 1974. It wouldn't be long before the two youngsters were to become arch rivals.

Bjorn began his Wimbledon run in 1976. He was playing well and won without much difficulty in the early rounds. The game was ready for some new young blood, as the likes of Laver, Rosewall and Newcombe were getting up in years. Bjorn fought his way into the semifinals where he whipped American Roscoe Tanner in straight sets. Now he was in the finals against temperamental Ilie Nastase of Romania.

Nastase was the Peck's Bad Boy of tennis, often throwing on-court temper tantrums that could unnerve an opponent, making gestures at fans and officials. He was also highly talented and playing some of the best tennis of his life. The writers were playing on the theme that this could be Nastase's last real chance to win at Wimbledon. In a strange way, he was a sentimental favorite. The twenty-year-old Borg would have other chances.

But Bjorn was on his game. Playing steadily with minimum errors, he forced Nastase to lose his cool. The young Swede hit deep and with authority, served well, and retrieved some of Nastase's best shots. He won the match and the Wimbledon title with seeming ease, 6-4, 6-2, 9-7.

Borg played even better tennis in 1977. It was now obvious

that he was close to being the best in the world, a spot Jimmy Connors had been claiming for himself for a couple of years already. People looked to Wimbledon '77 to perhaps settle the issue. After all, Bjorn had won Wimbledon '76, but Connors had come back to defeat the Swede in the finals of the U.S. Open later in the year. Then in January of '77, Bjorn whipped Connors in the Grand Slam final at Boca Raton, Florida. The rivalry was building up.

In fact, Connors, three years older, had beaten Bjorn seven of the first eight times they had met. But Bjorn was a growing boy then. Now, things seemed to be evening out.

Bjorn breezed through the early rounds, while Connors had some tough matches and was complaining of a bruised thumb. Then in the quarterfinals, Borg met Nastase again. He made it look even easier than the last year, whipping the Romanian bad boy 6-0, 8-6, 6-3. Connors also won in the quarters, then defeated eighteen-year-old John McEnroe in the semis. He was ready for the final.

For Borg, the semis weren't so easy. He went up against tough Vitas Gerulaitis of the United States in what turned out to be a classic match. The first set was close. Bjorn broke Vitas's serve once and that's all he needed. He closed it out with a service ace for a 6-4 win. But Gerulaitis came back to take the second, 6-3. Then Bjorn won the third by the same score, and Gerulaitis took the fourth by that same 6-3 margin. Both were playing extremely well, and they went into a fifth set.

They exchanged breaks early. Gerulaitis served to save the match twice, at 4-5 and 5-6. Both times he did it. But Bjorn's firepower finally prevailed and he won the set and the match. The final tally was 6-4, 3-6, 6-3, 3-6, 8-6. When it was over, an English broadcaster called it "the finest match for sustained brilliance over five sets I've ever seen at Wimbledon."

Now the question was could Bjorn regroup in time for Connors? In the first set it looked as if he couldn't. Connors came out firing and blasted twenty-one clean winners past Bjorn to take the set easily, 6-3. He looked sharp, while Borg looked to be tentative in his shotmaking.

Then perhaps came a turning point. In the third game of the second set Bjorn fought off four break points by blasting his much-improved first serve at Connors. He also began varying the pace of his strokes, throwing Connors off balance. He was using his head.

Suddenly it was Bjorn who was on fire. It was 2-2 in the second set when it happened. He took eight straight games and ten of the next eleven to win the next two sets, 6-2, 6-1. He had broken Connors's serve five straight times and completely turned the match around.

But Connors has never been a quitter. He pulled himself together. The forehand, his one weak link perhaps, was betraying him more than usual, so he went to his strengths, the backhand and serve, and pulled out the fourth set 7-5. Now it was a fifth and final set, Borg's second consecutive five-setter.

Bjorn seemed to get a second wind and swept through the first four games with relative ease. He looked to have the match put away. But again Connors rallied. He saved the fifth game, broke Borg in the sixth, held in the seventh, and broke Bjorn again in the eighth. Suddenly it was 4-4. Now Connors appeared to have the momentum and a grip on victory.

But then Connors seemed to lose his cool. He double-faulted, sent a backhander way over the baseline, and lost the game on a similar forehand. Bjorn had broken and was ahead 5-4. Now all he had to do was hold serve to win the match. And that's what he did, winning four straight points to take his second Wimbledon title, 3-6, 6-2, 6-1, 5-7, 6-4.

"I was never so tired in my life," Bjorn said, "but it was for sure my happiest win."

Later, when he talked to reporters, he said this about Connors.

"I used to give up like a little baby against Jimmy. I was scared of him. Now I am grown up and know I can hit the ball past him."

As for Connors, he was already looking forward to the

America's Jimmy Connors was
Bjorn's major rival for the world's
best ranking in the mid-1970s.
(United States Tennis Association)

next time. "Who is there but me and the Swede," he said.
"Sure, he's bigger and knocks the fuzz out of the ball. But
give me a good thumb to return serve with, and I'll kill him.
It's only me and him for all the marbles. Wait till next time."

So the gauntlet was thrown. Plus there was added pressure
on Bjorn in '78. He was trying to become the first three-time-
in-succession winner of Wimbledon since Fred Perry, and no
one would let him forget it.

Perhaps that's why he seemed nervous and unsure in his
opening match against big Victor Amaya. Through four
games of the fourth set Amaya was leading, 9-8, 1-6, 6-1, 3-1.
He just had to hold serve to run out the match. But Bjorn
pulled himself together and won the fourth set, 6-3, and the
fifth by the same score to take the match.

Then he settled down to play great tennis again. Those
who had followed his career said he was stronger than ever
and hitting the ball with greater authority and accuracy.
Connors was also playing very well. In the semis, Jimbo
whipped Gerulaitis 9-7, 6-2, 6-1, while Bjorn trounced Tom

Okker 6-4, 6-4, 6-4. So another Connors-Borg showdown was in the offing. And Connors would like nothing better than to be the man to stop Bjorn from getting three straight.

Connors won the first two games of the first set and seemed to be in control. Then it all went haywire. The match never approached the struggle of the year before. Trailing 0-2, Borg found his game and reeled off six straight to take the set. He allowed Connors just fifteen points.

From there it was a cakewalk. Bjorn won the next two sets 6-2, 6-3, to run out the match. When it ended, he gave a rare show of emotion, going to his knees and throwing his hands in the air. He had done it, three straight Wimbledons.

"I wasn't into the match mentally," was all a disconsolate Connors could say. Others said more, mainly that Borg had finally surpassed Connors in all-around skills and was now the best player in the world. They pointed to Bjorn's improved serve, which blasted out Connors. The Swede had won twenty-four points on serves that didn't come back across the net, including five aces.

"I know I serve better than Jimmy," said Borg. "I do not fear his serving and feel I can break every time. If I am serving well, I know I can break, because he doesn't serve well then."

Now there was talk of a Grand Slam. Bjorn had already won the French title in '78. Now he added Wimbledon. If he could win the U.S. Open and the Australian Open in December, he'd have the first Grand Slam since Rod Laver had done it in 1962 and again in 1969. Bjorn admitted he would go to Australia if he won the U.S. Open. But when Connors heard this, he bristled.

"I may follow him to the ends of the earth now," said Jimbo.

So they went to the U.S. Open, and who should meet again in the finals but Connors and Borg. This time it was Bjorn with a bad thumb, an infection beneath a blister. But those watching said it wouldn't have mattered. Connors came out like a tiger whose life was at stake. He hit everything Bjorn threw at him hard and straight, putting the ball wherever he wanted. It was his day and he beat Bjorn badly in straight sets, just as Bjorn had beaten him at Wimbledon. Once again the number-one ranking was up in the air and people took sides.

Their rivalry is so good for tennis and both know it. They're not really friends off court, but certainly don't dislike each other. There has to be a tremendous amount of mutual respect.

As of 1978, these two giants seem head and shoulders above the rest of the tennis world, perhaps their personal rivalry bringing each to even greater heights. And it should continue for years to come.

It's doubtful whether either one will emerge victorious in the long run, in other words, asserting complete dominance over the other. Both are winners, that's for sure. Each time they play in a final, it's a tennis event. But Borg's win at Wimbledon in 1978 has to be one of the great events of the 1970s. Since there are only two members of the three-straight-Wimbledon club, it's obviously a feat that doesn't come easy. It will be a long while before it happens again.

ABOUT THE AUTHOR

BILL GUTMAN is a free lance writer who has written both fiction and nonfiction in the sports field. He was born in New York City and grew up in Stamford, Connecticut. Mr. Gutman received a B.A. in English Literature from Washington College in Chestertown, Maryland, and has done graduate work at the University of Bridgeport.

He began his writing career as a reporter and feature writer for *Greenwich Time*, a daily newspaper in Greenwich, Connecticut. He later became the paper's Sports Editor. After a brief fling in the advertising field, he returned to writing full time.

Mr. Gutman has written books on all the major sports, including biographies of Pistol Pete Maravich, O.J. Simpson, and Hank Aaron. He's also written a biography of jazz great Duke Ellington. His fiction has appeared in Fawcett's baseball and football annuals, in *Boys' Life* magazine, and has been collected in a book published by Julian Messner. He presently makes his home in Wilton, Connecticut.